Turn Your
School Round

**A Circle-Time approach to the development
of self-esteem and positive behaviour in
the primary staffroom, classroom and playground**

TURN YOUR SCHOOL ROUND
LD 713
ISBN 1 85503 174 4
© Jenny Mosley
© Illustration Simon Barnes
Designed and produced by Chalk Layne Associates
Photography DLP Communications
All rights reserved
First published 1993

LDA, Duke Street, Wisbech, Cambs, PE13 2 AE

Thanks to Broadfields County Primary School, Harlow for their kind co-operation with the photography.

Contents

ACKNOWLEDGMENTS

I would like to thank the following: David, Meg and Sally, my children who have always shown great understanding and interest in my work.

Helen Sonnet, my secretary, who has creatively helped me shape the ideas for the book, Kay Hardwick who tirelessly and enthusiastically put the book in order and Norma Freegard who gave limitless practical support.

Olly Gooden and all the Wiltshire Primary Advisors who initially promoted all the ideas in the L.E.A. and all the schools across the country who persevered with the philosophy and the practice. Finally, my wonderful mum who always boosts my self-esteem!

FOREWORD

This book embodies some of the most important principles established by the Committee of Enquiry into Discipline in Schools set up in 1988 under my chairmanship. Our recommendations were published, as the Elton Report, in 1989.

A central group of those recommendations urged every school to develop a 'whole school behaviour policy' involving, and supported by, everyone directly involved with the school itself. This theme has been central to Jenny Mosley's work in the field and it is now central to her book. Her scheme embraces a number of our other recommendations as well.

It has been very encouraging to hear, from many witnesses, of the success of her work in improving good schools and "turning round" those in difficulty, as it endorses some of the Committee's most important findings. It therefore gives me great pleasure to commend her book to other teachers who may profit from her experience and advice.

The Lord Elton

PREFACE

Are any of these scenes familiar?

Mr. Jarvis moved quietly around the classroom glancing at the children's work. He noticed, with some amazement that Sam his 'problem child', was actually making an effort to produce a piece of work. "Well done Sam", he remarked to him, " You are doing that beautifully".

"No I'm not!" he snapped back, "It's rubbish". Pushing his work to one side he stared moodily ahead.

Sita woke up with a sickening feeling of dread; "Mum" , she called, "I don't feel well, I've got a tummyache, can I stay home today?" "Not likely – get up quickly." Sita dragged her heels all the way to school. As they reached the gates, Sita could see them waiting for her. As soon as her mother had left, she heard them shout "You keep away from Sarah and me. You're not our friend. Anyway, nobody likes you, you're a stupid cry baby."

Ahmed handed his mother the letter. She didn't need to read it – she knew what she would find – Ahmed was misbehaving, could she make an appointment with the headteacher? "I've never heard a good word about you , Ahmed, you're nothing but trouble."

Charlotte Johns, headteacher slumped over the driving wheel of her car. In a minute she would have to go indoors. Her husband would want some interesting conversation and her children would want her attention. What a day! The usual problems of staff back-biting, a queue of 'naughty' children a mile long outside her office, parents up in arms and now pressure from the governors. "Oh not now, Jane," she said as her youngest peered in the car window.

Molly the lunchtime supervisor, felt her temperature rising as she looked at the noisy rabble with mounting anger. "Shut up, you lot!" she yelled "or you'll be in trouble."
"Shut Up... I Said."

Sally entered the staffroom, ready to collapse into the nearest chair. She felt shell-shocked and tearful after another 'bout' with Alex. "Hello", said Peter, "What's your problem?"
"It's Alex Masters. He's so naughty in the classroom. I just don't know what to do with him." "Alex Masters!" said Peter, "Fancy that, he was great for me last year."

One disturbing factor that all these scenes share is that one person, probably with low self-esteem, is lowering the self-esteem of another, thereby affecting the whole ethos of the school.

I became interested in the concept of self-esteem when I started teaching over twenty years ago. One thing my long career has taught me, through many difficult lessons, is that at the heart of a good school is a commitment to the enhancement of adults' and children's self-esteem through supportive and positive relationships.

I was fortunate to work early on in my career in a special school where, we all adopted a circle approach as a forum through which to offer peer support thereby enhancing self-esteem and self-discipline in ourselves and the children.

Throughout my career in primary, secondary and special education I have continued to develop my own, Circle-Time model. When I started working in Wiltshire the Primary Advisers considered it to be so effective that they employed me as a freelance consultant to run initial self-esteem awareness raising days for their headteachers. I worked in many schools running Circle-Time Sessions with the children, teachers, teaching support staff, lunchtime supervisors and parents.

I now spend my time taking this unique Circle-Time model into schools throughout Britain, from small rural schools to large inner city schools.

This book is the result of my research and hard-won experience. It also includes policies, reports and written statements from schools who have been successfully putting all the ideas into practice.

Note to the teacher
For easy reference, worksheets in this book have been marked to indicate when they are Circle-Time Session plans (CTS), and when they are handouts (H).

Introduction

COMMENTS FROM CIRCLE-TIMERS

"Following our recent General Evaluation, comments were made by The Primary Advisor that relationships within the school at all levels were excellent; between teachers and teachers, teachers and children, ancillary staff and children, and children and children. This has got to be a result of the school involving everyone in formulating a whole school self-esteem and behaviour policy."

Headteacher

"I think this approach has enormous value in helping create a positive atmosphere. This makes for a more effective and successful school."

Teacher

" It is a good time for a chat and giving suggestions for things about school.

I like Circle-Time because we can discuss our problems and learn from our mistakes."

Pupil

"It has made me more aware of my faults."

"I will give children more of me."

"I have better understanding of children's needs."

Lunchtime supervisor

"The meeting really made me want to become more involved with the school to help my child. It gave me lots of ideas of how I could be more positive and supportive."

Parent

SELF-ESTEEM

Young or old, we all hold an inner picture of ourselves, of our strengths and limitations. This self-picture has been, and is, contributed to both by the positive and negative responses we receive from people who are important to us. Our self-image and the value we attribute to it then influences the way we respond to all life's challenges and choices.

If we have been encouraged and praised and have been given some opportunities to experience personal and social success we are more likely to perceive ourselves as capable, likeable and worthwhile people; in other words, we will have sound self-esteem. An adult or child with sound self-esteem will be confident in their ability to eventually succeed, will welcome and enjoy new learning experiences and will be able to relate well to other people. Their self-confidence and optimism will allow them to adopt a positive approach in all that they do and this will be effective in creating all manner of academic and social success. Moreover, sound self-esteem enables people to learn from criticism, and to view failures in a balanced and realistic way.

Sound self-esteem should not be confused with a seeming 'over confidence' which leads some people to continually claim how wonderful they are and to ride 'rough-shod' over others' feelings. People with sound self-esteem do not need to constantly tell people about their attributes; they are able to admit to mistakes and to listen sensitively to the needs of others.

An individual with low self-esteem is likely to view themselves as useless, unlikeable and incompetent. This lack of inner confidence can result in them constantly putting themselves down, an inability to relate in a warm, respectful and empathetic way to others and a fear of facing new learning experiences. Their personal view of themselves will lead them to believe that this is how others view them and will act defensively in order to protect themselves from further hurt. For example, by being the first to put other people down, by behaving aggressively, or by withdrawing into a 'shell'.

Secretly people with poor self-esteem regard themselves as failures, or as misunderstood and it seems to them that everyone is more capable than they are. This negative thinking results in a pattern of negative behaviour which becomes a self-fulfilling prophecy ensuring they continue to fail.

Fortunately, self-esteem is never a 'fixed' attribute, it can continually be influenced and enhanced. Children and adults alike have the same need for positive self-regard.

The problem with adults or children who suffer from low self-esteem is that they are very difficult to work with and relate to. Their self-protective behaviour means that they often avoid facing any situation in which they might fail. Ironically, they will refuse to recognise their own achievements, resent other people's successes, can delight in 'winding up' others, reject praise, humiliate others or refuse to respond to those around them at all. Such defensive, withdrawn, self-destructive or hostile behaviour, hurts, confuses or angers others, in turn lowering their self-esteem. If every encounter with that person is negative, then over time the recipient of that behaviour will reciprocate with the same aggressive and dismissive manner. Low self-esteem perpetuates itself and can drag others into the same vicious circle.

In schools, children and staff become trapped within this negative cycle of low self-esteem. With children it is often their initial poor or inappropriate behavioural responses that ensure they experience little or no learning or social success. They can perceive themselves as academically or socially inadequate and continue to be low achievers, 'switched off' and more likely to develop patterns of negative behaviour. At least this sort of behaviour guarantees them some attention; negative attention is better than nothing!

This pattern offers the low self-esteem adult or child some security as their presence is constantly acknowledged. They become reluctant to risk tackling any positive change in case it does not work. Risking change means allowing themselves to become vulnerable to entering the demands of relationships and facing new challenges.

The issue of self-esteem in pupils and staff alike is crucial to the effectiveness and happiness of a school and as such is far too important to be relegated to a half hour slot in a Personal, Social or Health Education Programme.

> The task of enhancing self-esteem is the most important facing any school.

REPORTS FROM HEADTEACHERS USING CIRCLE-TIME

We all work as a team (staff, children and helpers) to help each other when problems occur. This has involved the parents too. As a result, the attitudes of all concerned have changed considerably, becoming positive and supportive. I feel that we have a lovely, positive, caring atmosphere developing within the school. There is more respect between staff and parents. Also, I feel that parents see the staff as being more approachable and a partnership is developing between us.

Extract from Report from Berwick St. James School.

The class visits were all well received by the staff. The opinions expressed were that circle work was helping teachers to develop a more positive attitude to children and encourage a community feeling within the class. It helped to raise self-esteem and was a controlled situation for pupils and teachers. It revealed problems and worries and opened up a non-threatening approach in dealing with them. It made children feel more responsible for their own behaviour and their interaction with other children and adults. Circle work increased the awareness of other children within the group and the need for tolerance and support within peer groups. Children are perceptive of their needs and became aware that behaviour can be modified by their acceptance and sanctions.

Extract from Report from Pembroke Park School

As headteacher of this school I am totally committed to the ideas put forward by Jenny Mosley. Circle work is so positive as every child is valued. The children are much more aware of the needs of their peers and so value their peers much more highly. Relationships between child/children/teacher are greatly strengthened; in fact with this approach everyone grows together. Behavioural problems are reduced as the children are led towards more independent thinking and thus become more responsible for their own decision-making. The children are given the luxury of time and space to reflect upon their thoughts and actions alongside their privileged teacher. The circle games do so much to promote the listening and talking skills required by the National Curriculum.

Extract from Report from Woodlands First School

A WHOLE SCHOOL APPROACH TO BUILDING SELF-ESTEEM

Undoubtedly, there are individual teachers who recognise the importance of developing positive self-esteem in their students and work very hard to create an environment that is conducive to that. Similarly, there are many teachers in management positions who strive to encourage teachers they work with, very aware of how vital encouragement and praise are in such a draining and sometimes thankless job.

Such efforts are valuable and worthwhile but consider how much more impact could be made if every member of the school, whether child or adult, was committed to creating an environment where everyone was regularly listened to and encouraged, where a school made clear its commitment to finding ways of building relationships and giving respect and support to all its members.

The Circle-Time Approach provides a tried and tested framework for the development of whole school policy on self-esteem and positive behaviour. What is particularly noteworthy about this approach is that the policy is contributed to by every member of the school community, rather than being delivered from on high. As a result, there is a tremendous sense of ownership and commitment, because everyone knows they had the opportunity to influence and shape the policy.

In fact, schools that have promoted this approach have found that the actual process of developing the policy has been as important as the resulting policy outcome. Their experience has been that the process itself develops self-esteem, mutual respect and positive relationships. Continuing with the Circle-Time Sessions ensures that the policy aims are maintained. (An example of a whole school policy can be found on page 159-173)

In 1989, The Elton Report (Discipline in schools) was published by the government. It made many recommendations to schools regarding whole school behavioural policies. The Circle-Time Apporoach outlined in this book fully meets these recommendations:

Recommendation: Headteachers should promote the development of both management support and peer support within the staff team, and the professional development of its members.
Circle-Time Sessions build support and develop staff skills. They encourage participants to understand the social and academic needs of children.

Recommendation: Headteachers should, in consultation with governors, develop whole school behaviour policies which are clearly understood by pupils, parents and other school staff.

The model I use develops this theme further by asking every member of the school community to contribute to the policies of the school.

Recommendation: Schools should strike a healthy balance between rewards and punishments. Both should be clearly specified.

The incentives and sanctions policies developed through Circle-Time Sessions emphasise the importance of balanced reward and sanctions systems, which are clearly defined and used by all members of the teaching and non-teaching staff.

Recommendation: Headteachers and teachers should ensure that rules are applied consistently by all members of staff, but that there is flexibility in the use of punishments to take account of individual circumstances.

Through Circle-Time Sessions with all members of a school community, Golden Rules are drawn up and displayed for staff and children. The incentive and sanctions policies include provision for children 'beyond' this normal system, clearly detailing and explaining usage of the provision.

Recommendation: All parties involved in the planning, delivery and evaluation of the curriculum should recognise that the quality of its contents and the teaching and learning methods through which it is delivered are important influences on pupil behaviour.

Regular staff meetings to evaluate the progress of individual children are recommended.

Recommendation: provide a range of rewards accessible to pupils of all abilities.

The model that I use recommends that a checklist is kept by all teachers, to ensure that a 'baseline' of tangible rewards is given to all children, and that rewards recognise both academic and social success.

Recommendation: Headteachers and teachers should give pupils every opportunity to take responsibility and to make a full contribution to improving behaviour in schools.

Circle-Time is a fully democratic, all embracing model which provides the opportunity for children to put forward their views. It encourages children to take responsibility for their own behaviour and to suggest ways themselves for improving and maintaining good behaviour and relationships.

Recommendation: LEAs and governing bodies which employ school staff should ensure that midday supervisors are given training in the management of pupil behaviour.

Considerable emphasis is given, in this model, to improving lunchtimes and the importance of including lunchtime supervisiors in decision making and policy development. The model ensures that adequate guidance is given to supervisors on ways of improving lunchtimes, that they are provided with an effective incentives and sanctions system, and are seen as valued and important members of the school community.

SO WHAT EXACTLY IS CIRCLE-TIME?

Circle-Time is a democratic and creative approach used to consider a wide range of issues affecting the whole school community; teaching staff, children, support staff, parents and governors.

Industry calls this method, "Quality Circles" and has been using it since the 1960's to overcome the gulf that can develop between management and the shop-floor, leading to a 'them and us' attitude. The reputation for quality which Japan enjoys can be attributed largely to the widespread use of the approach.

> Typically, a circle meets once a week for one hour to consider quality problems. Mostly they will tackle problems at the 'earthy' end of the scale... they will make suggestions for solving them.

In the school setting, the Circle-Time method involves all participants sitting in a circle and taking an equal responsibility for the solving of problems and the issues that they have highlighted themselves. It operates within an agreed framework of guidelines, participants must take turns to speak, listen and bring their concerns or ideas to the circle. Individuals are given time both to volunteer their own concerns for group help and to offer help and encouragement to others.

The teacher adopts a facilitative role in order to encourage participants to feel that they too have the authority and control to solve the behaviour, learning or relationship problems that concern them. Initially one of the facilitator's tasks is to introduce a range of Circle-Time strategies that will encourage co-operation and honesty within the class or staff group.

Through subsequent discussion, the sharing of ideas and the building of relationships, the participants develop a whole school policy on self-esteem and positive behaviour which is endorsed by all members of the school community.

Circle-Time holds self-esteem building to be a central aim.

HOW CIRCLE-TIME ENHANCES SELF-ESTEEM AND POSITIVE BEHAVIOUR

The very act of sitting in a circle emphasises unity and equality, encouraging attitudes of honesty and trust. Taking it in turn to speak and join in the activities clearly conveys a message of authority and control to all participants.

The adoption of a facilitative rather than a authoritarian role encourages participants to feel that they have the authority and control to make a positive difference to the behaviour, learning and relationship problems within the school.

Participation in Circle-Time enables children to have a sense of belonging to a group they can trust. The group comes up with its own Ground Rules to help build a feeling of safety. As people's feelings and views are acknowledged and acted open, members are able to build a sounder self-esteem.

The structures and techniques within Circle-Time teach individuals to become more clear, direct and honest with each other. By learning to express their feeling in a calm way they are learning to develop assertive relationships and thus learn they do not have to resort to aggressive, manipulative or withdrawn behaviour in order to have their needs met.

Circle-Time by its effective use of a range of activities and structures, aims to motivate those involved into a willingness to share thoughts and feelings in a safe environment and to initiate a collective responsibility for the promotion of self-esteem and positive behaviour.

Circle-Time ensures that everyone feels valued as all personal and social achievements are elaborated on by the staff or class group.

Examples of Circle-Time Sessions are given in section 3.

> Self-esteem is hard to measure but when in Circle-Time one sees the children's faces and the realisation that they are loved and liked and that their peers remember their actions and value them, it all seems worthwhile. We feel that Circle-Time is a most important part of our work.
>
> *Self-Esteem and Positive Behaviour policy from Christ the King School*

REGULAR CIRCLE-TIME HELPS YOUR SCHOOL AND YOUR PUPILS

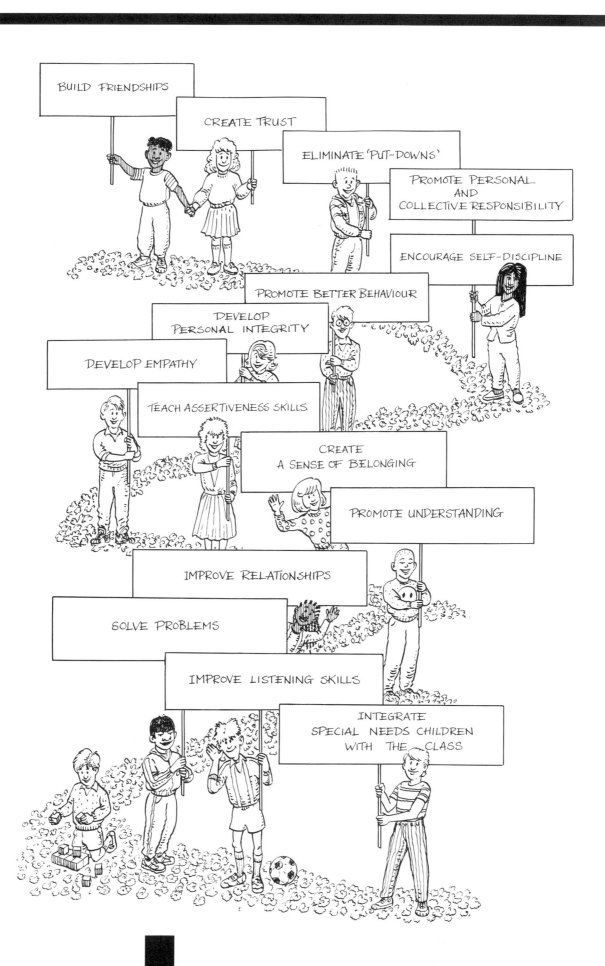

THE NATIONAL CURRICULUM AND CIRCLE-TIME

> How can we justify putting time and effort into Circle-Time when we have all the pressures of the National Curriculum to deal with?

This is a heartfelt and oft-asked question! The answer is really quite simple. Until children begin to feel positive about themselves, until good relationships are established and until there's a calm, safe, caring, well ordered environment, the national curriculum cannot be delivered effectively to all children. Over the years, research has constantly shown a direct link between the enhancement of self-esteem and the rising of academic achievement. Take the task of enhancing self-esteem as a guiding force in your school and children will begin to achieve their potential.

So, use of Circle-Time can be fundamental to pupils achieving academically as well as socially at school. It also meets quite specific requirements for the English National Curriculum. Pupils involved in Circle-Time will enhance their listening skills, and become thoughtful, coherent speakers.

Statements of Attainment

Pupils should be able to:

Circle-Time fulfils this requirement because:

Level 1

a) participate as speakers and listeners in group activities, including imaginative play.

a) games, rounds and drama ideas are promoted to encourage each child to join in.

b) listen attentively, and respond, to stories and poems.

b) many Circle-Time strategies are based on 'stories' which children develop, expand and discuss.

c) respond appropriately to simple instructions given by a teacher.

c) basic instructions for games rounds, are given.

Level 2

a) participate as speakers and listeners in a group engaged in a given task.

a) Circle-Time involves everyone in co-operative tasks.

b) describe an event, real or imagined, to the teacher or another pupil.

b) Circle-Time requires description of events from children's real or imagined life.

c) listen attentively to stories and poems, and talk about them.

c) Circle-Time helps children develop abstract ideas e.g.goodness, kindness, caring, from stories and poems.

d) talk with the teacher, listen, and ask and answer questions.

d) in Circle-Time issues are raised, not just with the teacher but also with each other.

e) respond appropriately to a range of more complex instructions given by a teacher, and give simple instructions.

e) initially instructions are given by the teacher but then the children are encouraged to 'take the lead' themselves.

Level 3

a) relate real or imaginary events in a connected narrative which conveys meaning to a group of pupils, the teacher or another known adult.

a) children are encouraged to talk through real events that have positively or negatively affected them. At other times they are encouraged to enjoy telling a fantasy story to their group.

b) convey accurately a simple message.

b) rounds often focus on giving simple messages to each other.

c) listen with an increased span of concentration to other children and adults, asking and responding to questions and commenting on what has been said.

c) further discussion on issues raised, between teacher and children encourage them to look for and develop themes.

d) give, and receive and follow accurately precise instructions when pursuing a task individually or as a member of a group.

d) Circle-Time strategies encourage children to 'take charge' and all take a turn at being leader.

Level 4

a) give a detailed oral account of an event, or something that has been learned in the classroom, or explain with reasons why a particular course of action has been taken.

a) children are given opportunities to relate events and discuss implications.

b) ask and respond to questions in a range of situations with increased confidence.

b) Circle-Time encourages questioning and responses by providing a safe, calm environment.

c) take part as speakers and listeners in a group discussion or activity, expressing a personal view on what is being discussed or experienced.

c) children are encouraged to put forward personal views and appreciate the value of being tolerant and accepting differences between themselves.

d) participate in a presentation.

d) develop a theme into a drama presentation.

Level 5

a) give a well organised and sustained account of an event, a personal experience or an activity.

a) Circle-Time offers each child the opportunity to develop coherent thinking and speaking.

b) contribute to and respond constructively in discussion, including the development of ideas; advocate and justify a point of view.

b) debating skills are enhanced and the merits of discussion are focused on.

c) use language to convey information and ideas effectively in a straightforward situation.

c) strategies encourage development of descriptive skills.

d) contribute to the planning of; and participation in, a group presentation.

d) strategies offer many opportunities for developing group work skills.

e) recognise variations in vocabulary between different regional or social groups, and relate this knowledge where appropriate to personal experience.

e) strategies focus on differences between individuals in many areas.

Level 6

a) contribute to group discussions, considered opinions or clear statements of personal feeling which are clearly responsive to the contributions of others.

a) Circle-Time strategies enhance development of reasoning skills.

b) use language to convey information and ideas effectively in a variety of situations where the subject is familiar to the pupils and the audience or other participants.

b) this area will have been focused on and developed through Circle-Time.

c) contribute to the planning and organisation of, and participate with fluency, in a group presentation or performance.

c) Circle-Time strategies offer many drama opportunities.

WHAT THE EXPERTS SAY

Comments made by children using Circle-Time

Comments made by teachers, parents and lunchtime supervisors using Circle-Time

TEACHERS

"It gives all children a chance to participate on an equal footing with both their peers and the teacher and raises their self-esteem when they realise that everyone's ideas are valid."

"I feel it gives children a better understanding of each other and of us as adults."

"It encourages the children to be self-controlled and to think of others in the class."

"It encourages children to take turns and develop the skill of listening."

"Circle-Time is practical, constructive, effective and confidence boosting."

"For the teacher benefits include a sounder knowledge of the class, a greater trust in the capabilities of the children, a wider knowledge of him or herself through the children and an opportunity for fun."

"It is an ideal opportunity to build on relationships – you have time as a teacher to concentrate solely on listening to the children."

PARENTS

"I now have lots of ideas on how I could be more positive and supportive."

"I must try harder not to ignore or put-down my daughter's opinions."

"It made me remember some of the anxieties of my own childhood that I'd forgotten."

LUNCHTIME SUPERVISORS

"I am now better prepared to deal with a crisis."

"I have a better understanding of children's needs."

"I have learned to be a better listener."

Section 1

A framework for a whole school approach

QUESTIONS TO ASK ABOUT YOUR SCHOOL

Teachers and pupils	Yes	No
Do you find that some 'labels' are constantly used for certain children e.g. lazy, naughty, stupid?		
Are the same children regularly appearing outside the headteacher's office?		
Are teachers using rewards and punishments in an inconsistent way?		
Are teachers consistently referring 'offenders' to other members of staff instead of managing the problems themselves?		
Are the tangible rewards offered by staff mainly for academic success, e.g. 'good work'?		
Do only a small percentage of children regularly receive 'good news' about themselves which goes home to their parents?		
Do the "middle-plodder" children get overlooked?		
Are the quiet children given enough individual attention?		
Do you listen to all the children's anxieties and fears about class time or play time?		
Do teachers encourage the children to take individual and group responsibility for their behaviour?		
Is there a system that allows children to record and monitor their own progress?		
Do staff have a regular and set time to discuss problems with individual children?		
Are the children involved in formulating behaviour policies?		
Do children often tell-tales?		
Are there often 'upsets' at lunchtimes that stop children settling down in the afternoon?		
Do some children 'dominate' others – i.e. other children only feel 'safe' if they're a part of that dominant child's 'gang'?		
Do special needs children get left out or picked on?		

Teachers and pupils	Yes	No
Do the children frequently call each other unkind names?		
Do some children frequently reject your praise?		
Are there some children who have withdrawn completely and have no friends?		
Are the children generally unsupportive and unhelpful to each other?		

Support staff and pupils	Yes	No
Do lunchtime supervisors use standing against the wall or sending them in' as their sole means of maintaining order?		
Do lunchtime supervisors regularly refer the same offenders to staff/headteacher?		
Do staff and lunchtime supervisors meet regularly to discuss problems?		
Do staff and lunchtime supervisors have an agreed behaviour policy?		
Have support staff been given the same sort of incentives and sanctions as the teachers?		
Are support staff involved with and included in the school behaviour policy?		
Do the support staff receive adequate recognition and support from the teaching staff?		
Do support staff have any meetings with the children to discuss behaviour and pool ideas?		
Are support staff encouraged to share the school ethos?		
Are all support staff given the opportunity to put forward ideas for improvement?		
Are support staff generally happy with their roles?		

Parents	Yes	No
Do the majority of parents show interest in and goodwill towards the school?		
Do staff regularly consider new or different ways to encourage parental interest and involvement?		
Are parents involved in formulating the behaviour policy?		
Are parental views actively canvassed in any way?		
Does the school promote any awareness raising for parents about self-esteem and the contribution they can make?		
Are parents actively encouraged to support and reinforce school behaviour policies?		
Are parents regularly informed of 'problems' which arise within the school?		

A WHOLE SCHOOL SELF-ESTEEM
AND POSITIVE BEHAVIOUR POLICY CYCLE

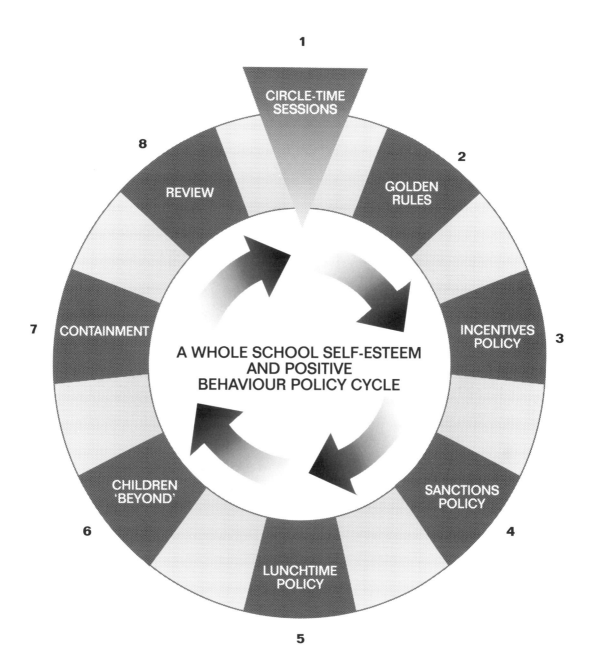

1 CIRCLE-TIME SESSIONS
2 GOLDEN RULES
3 INCENTIVES POLICY
4 SANCTIONS POLICY
5 LUNCHTIME POLICY
6 CHILDREN 'BEYOND'
7 CONTAINMENT
8 REVIEW

A WHOLE SCHOOL SELF-ESTEEM AND POSITIVE BEHAVIOUR POLICY CYCLE

DEVELOPING THE STAGES OF THE CYCLE

1 Circle-Time Sessions

Circle-Time Sessions are initiated for all staff and children to highlight areas of concern relating to relationships and behaviour within the school. Later, when people feel more confident they can offer them to parents. Initially Circle-Time Sessions are to encourage everyone's views and ideas and to promote a more caring and supportive environment enabling all members of the school community to feel secure and respected. Structures and strategies are chosen to encourage the personal development of all participants. From the ideas generated through initial Circle-Time Sessions, Golden Rules are discussed. **The process of sharing, discussing and negotiation is as important as the outcome.**

2 Golden Rules

Golden Rules are drawn up with children, staff and lunchtime supervisors to outline the explicit behaviours that show respect and caring towards one another. Golden Rules also incorporate physical safety measures. The relevant set of Golden Rules is displayed in each classroom, staffroom, dining hall and playground. The rules may not all focus on exactly the same issues, but nevertheless will fall broadly under the philosophical 'umbrella' of:

respect for myself

respect for others

respect for property

3 An Incentives Policy

Through continuing Circle-Time an Incentives Policy is now devised with the children and adults to promote and reinforce the Golden Rules. Eventually the intrinsic rewards offered by warm relationships and a stimulating curriculum are the ideal incentives. However, initially it is important to devise a tangible reward system which recognises all forms of social and academic achievement and regularly communicates this 'good news' to children and their parents. Care must be taken that social values such as kindness and politeness are given equal weight. The policy must ensure that every child experiences some degree of success and recognition and must, therefore, include a 'baseline' of incentives that every child has a right to receive. The incentives must be agreed on and used by all staff members of the school including lunchtime supervisors, so that a consistent approach is adopted. Children, too, should be able to nominate and award each other with the agreed incentives for any positive action or behaviour they have noticed in another child.

People need to be valued

All individuals need to receive regular praise and encouragement.
If children hear regular good news about their qualities and strengths, they are more able to work constructively on improving their weaknesses. Mistakes and criticisms can be handled by individuals who are convinced of their good points. Thus, individuals with sound self-esteem are more likely to work on improving their skills than those individuals who are threatened by yet more failure.

It is essential, therefore, that schools overhaul their Incentives Policy to ensure that all children receive regular 'good news' about themselves. When a child is given incentives, other people including peers and parents hear the 'good news' as well and correspondingly think and respond more positively toward that individual.

It is also important that schools do not overlook the fact that adults should also receive regular 'good news', praise, recognition and encouragement. If the adults' self-esteem is neglected they will not have the motivation and energy that is needed to take on the task of boosting self-esteem in others.

Although most teachers would agree with the idea of providing incentives to encourage children in their skills and attitude to their academic work, some can resist the idea of rewarding positive classroom or playground behaviour. They consider that such appropriate behaviour should be part of the 'norm' of school routine. However, as Circle-Time will reveal, negative behaviour results when a child's needs are not met, they are unhappy, or when they experience very different standards of behaviour at home.

Children, therefore, must initially be given tangible incentives to break inappropriate behaviour patterns, i.e. rewards should be given for politeness, consideration, sitting calmly, excellent listening and playing well with others. Once positive behaviour is established, the need for regular tangible incentives is reduced and intangible incentives such as positive relationships, success through the curriculum, verbal praise and positive self-evaluation soon become the most motivating factors and the intrinsic reward. However, this positive situation will only occur when behaviour has improved sufficiently to allow for a corresponding improvement and success in the learning environment.

Incentives should be shared by the whole school community. Everyone, including the children, should have access to the system. Circle-Time is a very useful setting for children in which to nominate each other for any of the school's incentives. Children should be able to put up their hand and choose someone to say "well done" to – someone who has stopped calling them a name or to someone who has been kind to them. Children should be able to nominate each other for stickers and certificates and be the one that actually hands them to the other child with a "thank you." The adherence to a whole-school policy on incentives provides a consistent approach throughout a school. At present, children often experience confusion as a result of the many and varied forms of incentives used by individual teachers. Once a policy has been formulated, the children are secure in their knowledge that a standardised system of rewards throughout the whole school will always notice their positive efforts.

Summary

❍ An Incentives Policy must have the consensus of and contributions from the whole school community if it is to be effective.

❍ All members of the teaching and support staff must agree with and act upon the policy.

❍ It is very important that all staff – teachers, supervisors, lunchtime supervisors and other support staff draw upon the same range of incentives and sanctions and are visibly seen by the children to uphold and support each other's decisions.

❍ To ensure that all children experience some success, a 'baseline' of incentives should be incorporated into the policy and a checklist (see below), kept for each child, on which staff record the tangible rewards that the child receives, ensuring that every child does reach the termly 'baseline'. Staff can award as much as they like in addition to the 'baseline', but every child in every class can expect to receive some reward for good behaviour as outlined in the Golden Rules.

❍ Parents should be informed of the incentives so that they can congratulate their children too.

EXAMPLE OF CHECKLIST FOR INCENTIVES BASELINE

Name	Sticker	Certificate	Responsibility	Congratulatory letter	Leaves for family tree
Mary Allen	✓ ✓ ✓	✓	✓ ✓ ✓	✓ ✓	✓
Peter Barnes	✓ ✓	✓	✓ ✓ ✓ ✓	✓	✓

Checklist for incentives 'baseline'

Every school should decide their own minimum baseline for rewards.
The school that devised the checklist above decided that each child should receive a minimum of 1 sticker, 1 certificate, 3 responsibility badges, 1 congratulatory letter, and 1 leaf for the family tree per term.

Some possible incentives –

Good work and good behaviour board:

Each child has an opportunity to display a piece of work s/he is pleased with for one day. The other children are encouraged to view and praise the piece. Children can also display a drawing of a particularly good behaviour that pleased them.

If the child has been particularly successful with some positive behaviour, they can either nominate themselves or be nominated by another – then a self-portrait or photograph can be placed on board with a halo on top with the particular behaviour written inside.

Smiley stickers:

'Smiley' faces can be drawn on circular stickers and given for any positive action in either work or behaviour. The children themselves can think of reasons for giving this award especially for other children who generally receive fewer awards.

Stickers:

There are a wide range of stickers commercially available which commend a variety of positive efforts such as kindness, co-operation and trying hard. Children can decide the guidelines for giving these rewards and even award each other under the supervision of the teacher and during Circle-Time. A 'sticker' book can be given to each child, in which stickers are placed with the appropriate date and reason for the award. These books can be taken home by the child at the end of each year.

Scrapbook:

Each child has a scrapbook in which items selected by the child or teacher of 'good' work and examples of 'good' behaviour can be placed (or photocopied).

Seal of approval:

Rubber stamps are available with a variety of messages e.g. Well Done, Thank You, in an attractive design. Children can also colour these in. You could also design your own school stamp with an outline of your school on it.

Labels:

Labels on which is written a simple sentence e.g. 'You are good at tidying up' can be given by staff or children.

Showing and telling about good behaviour and good work:

This can be done in groups, classes or assemblies. It should be about work and good behaviour. Children could also take good work efforts and stories of good behaviour to share with another teacher or special friend in a different part of school. The headteacher could have a regular weekly time and issue invitations to children who have worked well, but records need to be kept to ensure that every child gets a chance to be 'special'.

Responsibility badges:

All children should be given the opportunity to carry out a special responsibility and wear an appropriate badge in order to let them feel trusted. The responsibility could be for such times as giving out/collecting equipment, being in charge of 'special' toys box, helping in the dining hall, etc. The most motivating responsibility is to be given the task of helping other less able or younger children. All children could be given the chance, on a weekly rota system, of going down to younger children to listen to reading, to read, or to play a special game.

Certificates:

Certificates for any praiseworthy act are useful because they can be taken home to show parents.

Congratulatory stationery:

A note or letter is sent home with any child who has made a positive effort. The letter can also thank parents for their support, which in turn encourages parents to praise the child.

Thank You

Dunwell School
Worthy Lane
Higher Esteem

25 September 92

Dear *Mr and Mrs Brown*,

I am pleased to inform you that *Sarah* has shown a great improvement this term in her behaviour, and thank you for your support.

Yours sincerely

Mrs Tryhard

Mrs Tryhard

Coloured dots:

Children can be encouraged to acknowledge their own success. They can each be allowed one coloured sticky dot per week to place on a piece of work that they are pleased with. Children can also reward other children with this method. These can then be presented during Circle-Time with the child's reason as to why they have rewarded themselves. If it is good behaviour they are pleased with they can draw a picture of that behaviour and place a dot on it.

Happy family tree:

A large bare tree trunk and branches are cut out of card and fixed to a wall. Both adults and children write positive comments about each other onto 'leaves' which are stuck or stapled one at a time, onto the tree, so that it 'flourishes' with positive statements.

Beehive of Achievement:

Staff cut out simple hexagons of card which are then stapled together and create a 'beehive' effect on the hall or classroom wall. Children can write their name on the card and describe something they have achieved. Each card is signed by the teacher who also writes an endorsing comment.
Developed by Newtown School

Opportunities for non-teaching staff to praise:

Stickers or 'praise' books can be used by lunchtime supervisors, welfare assistants, secretary, caretaker etc.

Build success into all programmes of work:

Don't forget that one of the biggest incentives for children is the opportunity to succeed. In order to ensure that children are not frightened of failing, all programmes of work should be broken down into achievable steps.

Privilege-Time (or the Happy Half-Hour Policy):

This particular whole-school incentive model has proved to be very effective in many schools.

Privilege-Time or Happy Half-Hour is a regular slot of free time, during which pupils can choose a 'special' educational activity. This 'privilege' time is seen as a reward for all children who uphold the Golden Rules. Loss of this Privilege-Time can be used as an effective sanction. There are several benefits to Privilege-Time.

○ It upholds the Golden Rules and acts as an incentive for children to keep them.

○ It provides a safe framework as it demonstrates to children that there are immediate consequences for unacceptable behaviours.

○ It gives children the power of negotiation through provision of 'earning back' contracts.

○ It ensures that children who are normally 'good' are continually acknowledged and rewarded.

○ It encourages all children and their teacher to enjoy a relaxed, stress-free time together.

How to create a Privilege-Time:

Initially, the teacher sits with the children and draws up a list of activities which they suggest. Typical examples of these are:-

○ Bringing in my own educational game to play with a friend.

○ Using a game from the class privilege box. This box can contain educationalgames, activity books or special reading books which can only be used during Privilege-Time. These boxes can rotate, on a half-termly basis between classes.

○ Doing a special job for the teacher.

○ Extra special maths.

○ Finishing my work.

○ Helping to teach younger children in another class.

○ Using the computer.

These activities are written onto a large chart. Each week, well ahead of the actual Privilege-Time, the children sign their names up for the desired activity (if two children wish to play a game together they must sign their names next to each other and circle both names.)

Certain activities such as using the computer or helping younger children are very popular and will need to be allocated on a rota system.

Infant teachers often prefer to give their children a more regular, but shorter Privilege-Time. They too can have a special privilege box, dressing-up box or even a 'disco time'.

EXAMPLE OF PRIVILEGE-TIME CHART:

Activity	Using the computer	Bringing in my own game	Using class privilege box	Finishing my work	Going to another class to teach younger children
Wk1	John Sarah	Peter, Susan Paul, Jenny Michael	Sally May David Simon Michaela Mark	Helen Philip Jane Paula	
Wk2					
Wk3					
Wk4					
Wk5					

4 A Sanctions Policy

A Sanctions Policy is drawn up for any infringements of the Golden Rules. It concentrates on loss of privilege, thereby reinforcing the ideal of acceptable behaviour leading to reward, praise and encouragement. This policy must be adhered to by all staff.

A consistently applied, whole school policy on sanctions is helpful to both staff and children. Teachers, support staff, and lunchtime supervisors often resort to shouting or sarcasm as forms of punishment because they feel unsupported or powerless to enforce any appropriate sanctions.

A Sanctions Policy, as with an Incentives Policy, must clearly uphold the specified Golden Rules and, unless it is effective, breaking these rules can become an incentive in itself to gain attention. Once every child understands that if they keep to the Golden Rules they will receive privileges, these privileges can then be used as an effective sanction.

Using Privilege-Time as a sanction

Every time a child breaks a Golden Rule e.g., shouts out, is unkind to another child, a written warning is placed on the blackboard or beside the child. If certain children use the warning system as opportunities for a 'free kick' they will lose that chance. If the child then breaks another Golden Rule his/her name is entered on a chart showing five minutes loss of Privilege-Time for each misdemeanour. Names can be entered on the chart as initials to save space.

Privilege-Time	Date	
5 min S.L. LR. J.O. P.B. D.B	**10 min** S.L. D.B. L.R.	**15 min** L.R.
20 min	**25 min**	**30 min**

A system of 'earning back' lost time should be introduced as encouragement for those children who are liable to lose all of their Privilege-Time and records should be kept of these agreements.

EXAMPLE OF AN 'EARNING-BACK' TIME AGREEMENT:

I agree to..(target)

in order to earn back...(min)

Signed Pupil...

Signed Teacher...

date..

It is often amazing (and wonderful!) how many children will set themselves difficult targets in order to 'earn back' Privilege-Time. It is both a positive and a motivating opportunity for a child to negotiate his/her own target.

During the loss of Privilege-Time it is useful to have 5 or 10 minute timers available, which a child can set for him/herself. Whilst the timer is in operation the child should sit quietly, observing the other children enjoying Privilege-Time and reflecting on what it means to break the Golden Rules. When his/her 'lost time' is completed, the child can join in the activities of Privilege-Time. Many schools testify to the success of this system.

Unacceptable behaviour

In those cases of extremely destructive behaviours, such as deliberate physical or verbal attacks on others, a definite policy should be agreed on by the staff. Other children and the child who has lost self-control need to know these situations cannot be tolerated. Withdrawal from the playground, or classroom and a written warning to the child and/or parent is needed. Obviously, a child who is resorting to this 'lashing-out' behaviour is disturbed and unhappy. It may be appropriate after carrying out this routine procedure, to then consider the contracting strategies suggested in the 'children beyond' section.

The policy must provide lunchtime supervisors with effective incentives and sanctions and include ideas for games and activity choices. The policy should seek to promote the status of lunchtime supervisors as important and worthwhile members of the school community and must, therefore, be upheld and reinforced by all members of staff and made clear to all parents.

Bored or bad behaviour:

> Since implementing a lunchtime policy the lunchtimes have improved beyond recognition. This is not an exaggeration, the supervisors are happier and the children are working more together. There are confrontations but nothing like the first year.
>
> *Combe Bissett School.*

Lunchtimes are one of the most influential and important times in a child's school day. It is a time when they are free to form friendships, to structure their own play and to exert self-discipline and responsibility towards others away from the structured environment of the class. The reality, however, is that many lunchtimes are a great source of stress for the heads, teachers, supervisors, and children. If these stresses and concerns are not aired and dealt with the problems can become extreme and adversely affect the relationships, behaviour and learning in a school. The first task is for schools to take on the lunchtime period as a communal responsibility and not just the responsibility of the supervisors.

Unfortunately many teachers have developed an insular and negative attitude towards lunchtimes:

> I've managed to control behaviour in my class – I really don't want to know what's happening outside – it's just one extra pressure too many.

Hopefully if Circle-Time Sessions for teachers are working well then attitudes will have mellowed and teachers would have become very aware of children's needs for emotional and physical safety, but it still may be necessary to bring the staff round to the view that the whole school needs to focus on these issues. This can be done by a communal inset day on "promoting positive behaviour" and inviting all the supervisors, educational assistants, parents, governors and teachers and maybe, even pupil representatives from the school council to attend. A useful trigger for circle discussion is to give out the handout "Problems during lunchtime," page 76 to teachers and ask if they can identify any problem areas that apply to their school. It will soon become clear that if these problems do exist, only a whole school effort can sort them out. A Circle-Time Session with the teachers based on "A lunchtime supervisors point of view" page 78 also helps teachers to focus in an empathetic way on the problems faced by supervisors.

6 Children 'Beyond'

There are some children who are 'beyond' normal incentives and sanctions and lunchtime policies, but you cannot, in fairness, name them until you have been operating these policies consistently for some time. These children are often confused children, whose basic emotional or physical needs have not been or are not being met. Within many of them there is a level of inner chaos which results in an absence of any internal boundaries. Often home itself fails to provide any limits. Consequently, these children are unable to recognise any of the normal boundaries of behaviour proposed by school; they are too unhappy, angry or suffering from low self-esteem. Their only way to regain any feeling of personal power is to wind other children or adults up. Because of low self-esteem they do not believe they have the chance of being 'good', so don't even bother to try. Once the normal system has been operating for sometime, it is easy to see who these children are as they are unable to respond to usual systems that motivate other children. It is important to help these children identify a small achievable target so that they can then experience success. They are often afraid of their own behaviour and don't believe they are able to regain control. An achievable target, accompanied by an agreed-on motivating reward can help them break out of their negative pattern. The teacher or lunchtime supervisor can suggest the use of a special contract. The child and adults need to agree on one target of achievable behaviour and agree on regular monitoring of the target and specific regular rewards that would motivate each particular child.

> Examples of particular rewards that have been effective are: helping the caretaker, working with younger children, special responsibility e.g. answering school telephone, special letter to chosen adult e.g. grandparent.

It is important to note that this type of individual contracting can only be effective if all other children regularly receive rewards and privileges because once they are, their support can be enlisted in helping a child identify and achieve his/her target and motivating reward.

Contracting can follow a certain procedure. Initially a teacher or another child can request a contract with a child 'beyond'. If it is lunchtime behaviour that is the problem then the contract must be made with the child, teacher and lunchtime supervisor working together. If, after running this contract for a while, progress is still poor, it will be time to bring in parents. Once the parents have agreed to a contract and to monitor progress, any failure of the child to reach his/her target can result in the option for the school to suspend the child from lunchtimes.

☆ ☆ ☆ ☆ ☆

I agree to be gentle and not physically hurt another child at lunchtimes. For every lunchtime I achieve my target I will receive a star on my card. Each star means that I have 10 minutes special time to help Mrs Jones with her younger children. If I receive 5 stars in one week I get a letter sent home which tells my parents how well I have done.

Pupil...

Teacher..

Lunchtime Supervisor...

Parent...

Monday	Tuesday	Wednesday	Thursday	Friday
☆	☆	☆		

EXAMPLE OF CLASSROOM CONTRACT:

I agree to stay on-task when the 5 minute timer is placed beside me.

If I stay on-task I will get a star on my card.

The teacher can choose or I can choose when I want to use the 5 minute timer. If I get 3 stars I get to use the computer with my friend for 10 minutes every day.

Pupil..

Teacher..

Parent...

The most difficult aspect of this strategy is for the teacher not to abuse the power of the contract. When harassed and angered by these children the teacher can tend to break the agreement. For example, if a child has completed this contract by staying on-task for 5 minutes successfully and then hits a child their star cannot be taken away from them – only the agreed sanctions can prevail. It is crucial therefore that the child also understands that the normal sanctions will prevail for certain unacceptable behaviours. Examples of such sanctions might be being moved away from a friend to work on their own, being sent to work in a different class, or staying in at breaktime.

It is important to keep the idea of rewards given to children for achieving targets, separate from privileges which can be removed when unacceptable behaviour occurs. This ensures that the child's experience of success isn't undermined by other behaviours. In this way, their self-image can be steadily enhanced.

It is important that parents are talked through the notion of 'contracting' to help them agree that they will not impose any punishments should the child not receive their reward. The emphasis is on reinforcing the positive behaviour. The misbehaviour will still receive the usual sanctions but these are applied by the school and not the parents.

As soon as the child reaches the contract stage any incident must be noted and logged in case any mental health professionals, such as educational psychologists, counsellors or play therapists need to be contacted. Where it is obvious that, despite the consistent efforts of outside agencies, the school can do nothing more to help the child, then the school can safely say they have reached the containment and staff support stage.

Withdrawn children

There is another group of children 'beyond', whose problems, whilst equally severe, may be overlooked because they are of a less disruptive nature. These are children who have become very withdrawn thereby indicating that they have given up asking for their needs to be met. Sometimes, their withdrawn behaviour makes it impossible for them to relate successfully to other children or adults as they remove themselves from facing any learning or social challenge. They are unlikely to contribute in the normal way to Circle-Time and need specialised help in order that the problem does not become so acute that it leads to depression or in extreme cases, a child becoming an 'elected-mute'. A withdrawn child may be helped to respond during a Circle-Time by whispering his/her contribution to a puppet, which the teacher then translates to the rest of the class and thereby acts as a go-between. Alternatively, a withdrawn child could be informed of the theme of a round prior to the Circle-Time e.g., my favourite meal, my best toy and could provide a picture rather than speak.

Particular attention must be taken to discover any interests or hobbies of a withdrawn child so as to use these as a basis for encouraging participation and a meeting with parents might be of benefit in discovering such areas of interest. It may also be necessary to involve outside help like the child and family guidance clinic, play therapists or counsellors to find ways of breaking the negative pattern of withdrawal.

7 Containment

Where all viable systems have failed to bring about any significant improvement in a child's behaviour and the stark reality is 'containment' it is important that an appropriate Action Plan is formulated by all members of staff. Adequate support must be given to the child's teacher, so that s/he is not left to struggle on alone and the other children are not adversely affected by the continual disruptive behaviour of that child and a harassed teacher. Other members of staff can offer practical support to allow 'time-out' for either the child or the teacher. Supervised, practical tasks can be given to the child, e.g. sticking stamps on the school mail, helping the caretaker in simple jobs, or the child could spend some time working in another classroom. It is most important that the self-esteem of the teacher and other children is not drastically lowered by the child's behaviour.

All policies need 'fine-tuning'

A termly Circle-Time review of the self-esteem and positive behaviour policy is important to keep the momentum going and prevent any 'sloppy' practice from creeping in. Any inconsistencies in the policies can be ironed out and improvements suggested once the staff have experience of the policies in action. "Plan-Do-Review" is a good axiom! Regular Circle-Time Sesions will also ensure that the whole staff continue to enhance their personal and professional development.

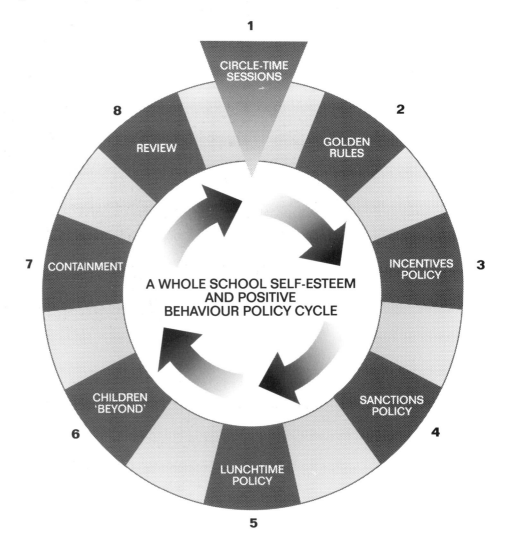

MODEL OF AN EFFECTIVE SCHOOL

A model to show how Circle-Time develops an effective school

Circle-Time Sessions are initiated to help
children and adults understand the concept
of self-esteem and its relevance to behaviour,
learning and relationships.

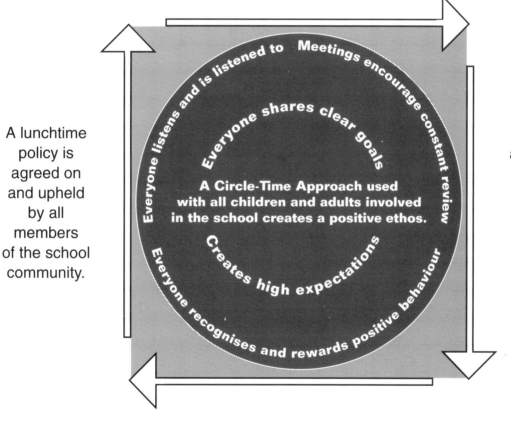

A lunchtime
policy is
agreed on
and upheld
by all
members
of the school
community.

Golden Rules
are formulated
through
Circle-Time,
written
up by and
given to the
whole school
community.

Everyone listens and is listened to   Meetings encourage constant review

Everyone shares clear goals

**A Circle-Time Approach used
with all children and adults involved
in the school creates a positive ethos.**

Creates high expectations

Everyone recognises and rewards positive behaviour

Incentives and sanctions policies
are developed and contributed by the children
and all the adults to uphold all the positive
behaviours outlined in the Golden Rules. All
adults and children are encouraged to use
these policies equally.

Section 2

Circle-Time Sessions for:

- **headteachers**

- **teachers**

- **educational support staff**

HOW TO RUN INITIAL CIRCLE-TIME SESSIONS FOR STAFF

The following section contains some outline programmes for initial Circle-Time Sessions. Once these programmes have been worked through they will create a safe framework for important issues to be explored. The suggested structures will also help the facilitator to feel more confident about taking on this approach. Please remember, however, that as trust between all the participants builds up, the format of the circle meeting, whether with staff or children, need not be so formal or prescribed. Flexibility and openness are the key qualities of a good circle facilitator. Facilitators are not there to push through their own ideas, they must develop their own listening skills in order to develop a true sensitivity to others' concerns and needs. The following Circle-Time Sessions have been created to help adults share the same foundation of understanding and commitment for self-esteem, which will then create the right climate for truly democratic circle meetings to develop at a later stage.

> It is vital that these Circle-Time Sessions take place within a school ethos that actively demonstrates a genuine caring for all staff members.
> There must be a congruence between respect generated by Circle-Time Sessions and respect for staff throughout the whole school day.

DO WE, THE ADULTS, NEED CIRCLE-TIME?

Often staff behaviour can be as bad as children's behaviour. Until we promote better relationships, behaviour and self-esteem for the staff, how can we promote it in children? The following checklist may help you focus on areas of difficulty.

Assessing the self-esteem & behaviour of the staff	
Do staff generally avoid the staffroom because it lacks an agreeable atmosphere in which to relax?	
Is 'backbiting' a common feature amongst the staff?	
Is there a general lack of support and helpfulness between members of staff?	
Is staff absenteeism a serious problem?	
Do members of staff lack the opportunity to put forward their views?	
Are 'put downs' about each other commonly used as a means of criticism?	
Do staff rarely experience praise from each other and from the headteacher?	
Is sarcasm or cynicism a common feature?	
Do the staff lack time to reflect on their success/achievements informally or formally through staff meetings?	
Do the staff rarely have social occasions in which to relax and enjoy each others company?	
Do the staff feel unable to consult other staff members about problems?	
Are senior members of staff considered unapproachable for help/advice?	
Do staff frequently grumble about their workload/responsibilities?	

IDEAS TO HELP RAISE THE SELF-ESTEEM OF STAFF

GUIDELINES FOR ALL CIRCLE-TIME SESSIONS

○ All participants sit in a circle with the agreed leader. This leader may well be the headteacher, but as confidence grows, any member of staff may choose to take on this task.

○ Initial sessions could usefully focus on the drawing up of agreed guidelines for staff behaviour, both within and outside the circle. There are certain Golden Rules within the circle that will need to be absolute, for example:

Do respect other people's rights to speak up – Don't use put downs

Do listen well – Don't interrupt when someone else is speaking

○ Circle-Time Sessions should occur on a regular basis at least once a half-term, with good communication in advance so that everyone knows they are happening.

○ The role of leader is to facilitate a supportive climate during Circle-Time Sessions, rather than to control and dominate. In this context the leader needs to be sensitive and perceptive in order to identify and elicit everyone's needs and points of view.

○ The leader must aim to encourage a feeling of positive co-operation and trust within the circle to enable the group to develop. It is essential that leaders take their turn and are honest in their contributions.

○ The focus or themes of the Circle-Time should take into account the current concerns and anxieties of the participants. Every session must include a positive focus, for example, the formulation of an action plan or the celebration of an individual or collective success.

○ Circle-Time Sessions must be seen as positive forum which will benefit all participants and enhance self-esteem, group work skills, good communication and creative and positive thinking.

GOLDEN RULES FOR STAFF

> We believe that rules should be set out in a positive manner. Staff have a set of Golden Rules for themselves and each class has negotiated Golden Rules for themselves.
>
> *From a Self-Esteem Policy, Margaret Stancombe Infants School*

Aim To raise awareness of the importance of respectful, caring relationships amongst staff and to help staff contribute to relationship guidelines they would be prepared to adhere to.

Round Ask each member of staff to think of any past INSET in which another person's behaviour upset or annoyed them. Typical answers include: someone dominating the conversation, being constantly interrupted whilst talking, being 'put-down' by someone, not being allowed sufficient time to state views/opinions.

Brainstorm During this round put these statements onto a flip chart under the title 'Golden Rules for Staff'.

Find a 'positive' for each identified 'negative' behaviour.

EXAMPLE

Do	Don't
allow others time to speak	dominate discussion
consider different views	be dogmatic
respect confidentiality	show lack of integrity
give eye contact and comfortable body language	use negative body language
be sensitive to other people's needs	disregard other people's needs
take responsibilty for your own behaviour/circumstances	blame other people or circumstances

GOLDEN RULES FOR STAFF

Question	Can we agree to adopt these rules for the way we act towards each other?
Pairs	In pairs now consider Golden Rules for adults' behaviour towards children.
Brainstorm	Put statements concerning guidelines for adults' behaviour towards children onto a flipchart as before.
Handout	**Golden Rules for myself.** Facilitator emphasises how difficult it is to find the energy to build relationships with others if we don't look after ourselves.

GOLDEN RULES FOR ADULTS WITH CHILDREN

Do	Do not
listen, make time for them	make them look stupid by asking them too hard a question or by ridiculing them
value and respect what children say and do	undermine opinions or feelings or interrupt them
distance the child from the fault	confuse the child's personality with the poor result
be consistent	change the goal posts
challenge the child to develop his/her personality/abilities	do it for them
be sympatheic and care about them	ignore them/dismiss their ideas
encourage them to support each other	let them put each other down

This example is taken from Self-Esteem policy-Newtown School.

Ending Round	Once everyone has read the handout, each person states One Golden Rule I am good at – One I need to work on.

Golden Rules for Myself

○ I should give myself the same care and attention that I give to others.

○ I am not an endless 'resource' for others. I must stock up on 'reserves' and not get too drained.

○ I have needs too, which may be different from my family's, my friends' or my colleagues'.

○ I do not have to say 'yes' to all requests or feel guilty if I say 'no'.

○ The 'perfect' person does not exist, making mistakes is permissible; I can learn from them, as can others.

○ I can't solve all the problems I'm confronted with. I can only do my best.

○ I have the right to be treated with respect as a worthwhile, intelligent and competent person.

○ I do not have to have everyone's approval all of the time to know that I am trying my hardest.

○ Time for unwinding is time well spent.

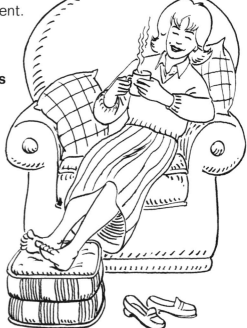

Select one of these Golden Rules to work on for yourself. You may wish to expand on it to suit your own personal need.

CTS

Aim To raise awareness of how children or adults who are given negative labels can become trapped within a negative cycle of failure.

Handout 1 Participants are each given a handout **The Vicious Circle**. The facilitator explains each stage of the cycle and asks the question "Can we think of any children who have acquired a negative label or whose behaviour has become stereotyped by adults or children in the school?"

Pairs In pairs, the participants are asked to choose one child who they feel has been 'labelled' or 'stereotyped' and work out an Action Plan which will break into the negative cycle of failure.

Reporting back Each participant reports back on the Action Plan that s/he has formulated.

Handout 2 A second handout, **The Positive Circle** is given to each participant.

Discussion The facilitator initiates discussion on the two circles and the group decides how to incorporate the necessary positive points into their behaviour policy.

The vicious circle

Negative labelling

Labels and stereotypes begin to be used frequently for certain individuals, e.g. stupid, naughty, bully.

Reinforced stereotypes

Poor performance and behaviour reinforces the poor self-image and negative view from others. Everyone feels justified in having given the original label.

Poor self-esteem

Individuals begin to develop a poor self-image. The label spreads to other children & adults in the class, staffroom and playground. Others start to hold this individual in poor regard.

Deteriorating skills

The lack of opportunities to practise different behaviours leads to their academic and social performance skills becoming poorer.

Low expectations

The individual's poor self-image creates low expectations from self and from others.

Fewer chances

Because of their reputations, these individuals are not offered the sort of opportunities that would bring social or academic success.

The positive circle — disregard any previous negative labelling and follow an agreed policy of positive feedback

Positive feedback

Agreed decision to give positive feedback on academic or social strengths.

Reinforce the more positive self-image

Improved performance skills reinforce better self-image and the concept of positive feedback from others.

Improved self-image

This leads to enhanced self-image in individuals and others notice an improvement in certain aspects.

Improved performance

More opportunities allow the individuals to practise and enhance their academic and social skills.

Higher expectations

Improved self-image creates higher expectations of self and from others.

More opportunities

Individuals are then trusted with more opportunities that will bring social or academic success.

THE NEEDS OF CHILDREN AND ADULTS

Aim To raise awareness of the effects of neglected needs on the self-esteem of individuals, to help adults understand the inner worlds of 'problem' children and to stimulate informed discussion on the needs of specific children through the use of Maslow's model.

Handout 1 **Maslow's hierarchy of human needs** is given to each participant. The facilitator highlights each stage of the triangle and asks the question "Do we know any children in this school stuck at this level? Are there any new plans we need to make to help meet children's needs?"

Handout 2 In pairs, each person takes time to explore the 'inner world' of one 'problem' child from their class using the Maslow model as the structure for discussion. Then they formulate an Action Plan to deal with the problems with the help of handout 2, **Some Questions using the Maslow model.**

Reporting Back Each participant reports back on the Action Plan they have devised to help that child.

Question How far is 'bad' behaviour a cry for help from an adult or a child unable to express the hurt they feel as a result of not having their needs met?

Would it help if we stopped using the negative phrase 'attention-seeking' and changed it instead to the more positive one of attention-needing?

Discussion If a child's or adult's needs are not being met then they are disempowered. Disempowered individuals get back power by subversive means, e.g. children bully, adults shout etc.

Reflection Can we channel any of the learning inspired by this session into written statements to put in our whole school self-esteem and positive behaviour policy?

Note: *All questions on handout 2 can be adapted and applied to the needs to adults in the school.*

Maslow's hierarchy of human needs

A child or adult cannot hope to have their needs met all the time by home or school, but if the needs of each stage are not met by either one or the other then that person will not be able to progress to the next level towards self-fulfilment.

Stage 1   Everyone needs food, warmth and shelter. We must consider how far lack of provision of the basic needs is affecting a child's behaviour and learning. For example, many children come to school without breakfast and insufficient lunch, many children's 'shelter' is under threat of repossession, many children have undetected hearing or sight problems, and so it goes on.

Stage 2   Everyone needs a safe and secure physical and emotional environment in the home, the classroom and in the playground. As long as adults and children feel safe somewhere, they can cope. Any type of verbal or physical bullying or harassment creates high levels of 'unsafety'.

Stage 3   We all have a need to be accepted, feel a sense of belonging and enjoy friendships. Some children feel unloved at home and isolated at school.

Stage 4   Everyone needs self-esteem; they need to feel good about themselves, to receive recognition, attention and appreciation.

Stage 5   Realisation of inner potential – this is the need we have for opportunities to develop all our inner talents and potential. All children and adults must be given chances to experiment with their own ideas and feel free to do their 'best'.

Some questions using the Maslow model

Stage 1　Do certain children frequently come to our school tired or hungry? How far do these factors contribute to the bad behaviour?

Do we need to send a letter as part of our health education programme to parents reminding them of the importance of sending a balanced lunch?

Do we need a snack policy for playtime?

Stage 2　Do we have enough listening time for children?

Do we know each child well enough for them to be able to tell us if something has gone wrong at home?

Are our children emotionally and physically safe enough in this school – in classrooms and the playground?

Have we a whole school behaviour policy incorporating emotional and physical safety rules?

Stage 3　Does this child receive sufficient affection and friendship?

Do we need to do more through the curriculum to promote the ideal of good friendship?

Have we got the Golden Rule 'Do ask people to join in, don't leave people out'?

Stage 4　Do we ensure that every adult and child in the school community receives praise, recognition and encouragement?

Do we have a policy on self-esteem to ensure that every child feels special and valued?

Do we all use incentives or is it just the teachers?

Stage 5　Are there opportunities for all children to discover their inner potential and creativity?

Are all children given opportunities for self-directed learning/reflective discussion and solving of problems.

Aim To help staff realise that their self-esteem is crucially important. If staff have poor self-esteem they lack the energy and commitment to effectively help each other or the children.

Round Ask each participant to think of and say one good and one bad thing that has happened to them that day.

Discussion Did any of these events or conversations lower or raise their self-esteem? Why?

Round Ask participants to think of one physical symptom that they suffer when feeling 'down' e.g. headache, tiredness, irritability.

Question Given that teaching can lead to a lowering of self-esteem and a mounting spiral of stress (Elton Report) what do we need from each other in order to survive? (e.g. support, honesty, trust, openness), and for ourselves (e.g. make 'treat ' time, physical exercise, see friends).

Pairs Decide together on an individual Action Plan for each partner that will give them some time and a sense of being cared for.

Action Plan In a circle together, formulate a positive Action Plan for whole staff self-esteem, (a typical example is provided on the handout).

STAFF SELF-ESTEEM – TEYFANT SCHOOL'S ACTION PLAN

Guideline	Immediate/ Medium term	Action	Action taken (✓)
1. Classroom a) More circulation staff doubling up/exchange classes for stories etc. b) Visits from the H.T. to offer constructive criticism and support.	M M	1. Discussion -Year Groups. 2. Staff to sign list if willing to exchange. 1. To be discussed by staff and on a 1:1 basis.	
2. Staff Meetings a) To be held in different room in school – different classes to formally 'invite' teachers to their rooms. b) To be held occasionally outside school in pleasant areas – perhaps where good teas can be served. c) Smaller groups for discussion where appropriate. d) Non-teaching staff invited to attend all meetings. e) Golden Rules to be drawn up and adhered to.	I M M I M	 1. Liaise to find other venues for Summer term (GPG). 1. To be included in plans for future meetings. 1. To be agreed by all staff.	

3. Staffroom
 	
a) Ground rules:-
 	
  (i) Talk to staff who feel isolated.
 	
  (ii) No 'put downs'.
 	
  (iii) Avoid cliques.
 	
  (iv) Peer support – more effort to praise each other.
 	
b) Establish a staffroom committee.
	I
	
	M
		1. Agreement by all staff.
		
		1. Reps. to be elected from Yr. groups (7/3/91).	

Guideline	Immediate/ Medium term	Action	Action taken (✓)
c) Buffet lunch once a fortnight for all staff.	M	1. To begin in the Summer term (discuss with Sally.)	
d) Coffee and cake for all staff on Fridays.	M	1. To be arranged by staffroom committee.	
4. Individuals a) No gripes without a willingness to suggest and accept change.	I		
b) Accept responsibility as an individual.	I		

STAFF SELF-ESTEEM – PART 2

Aim   To help individuals to build a more positive self-image. To raise awareness of the difficulties of being positive about ourselves.

Handout 1   Give each participant a copy of Handout 1, **You are the most important person; Your self-esteem is crucial.**

Pairs   In pairs, *both* are asked to concentrate on answering the questions for one partner at a time.

Discussion   Facilitators asks participants how difficult was it to be positive about themselves, and raise the point that our British culture tends not to encourage people to make positive statements about themselves or to each other. This makes it more difficult for adults to promote a positive self-esteem policy within a school.

Question   How can we have the energy and will to enhance others self-esteem if we don't use positive thinking for ourselves?

Handout 2   Give each participant Handout 2, **Some Golden Rules for myself.** Ask each of them to select one Rule which they particularly need to work on.

Action Plan   To enhance self-image by learning to make positive statements about oneself.

You are the most important person
Your self-esteem is crucial

Discuss the following statements as honestly as you can with your partner. Try to think of one thing for each category that has pleased you or makes you feel good about yourself.

1 Anything I have achieved at work or at home.

....

2 Any skills or aptitude that I possess.

....

3 Any special task which took a great deal of effort.

....

4 Anything I do which is of benefit to others.

....

5 Any character trait I like about myself.

....

6 Any obstacle or fear I have overcome.

....

7 Any habit or practice I have been able to change.

....

8 Anything I have said or written.

....

9 Any aspect of the way in which I relate to other people.

....

10 Any hobbies.

....

List the three things which have boosted your self-confidence, then three things you would like to feel more confident about.

Children also should be able to make positive answers to some of these statements, if our teaching methods are positive.

Some Golden Rules for myself

These will keep you within an upward cycle of good self-esteem in your own life.

○ I am not an endless 'resource' for others; I must stock up on 'reserves' and not get too drained.

○ I can't expect everyone to like me – after all, I don't like everyone I meet.

○ I have strengths to offer if I choose to.

○ I have achieved some positive things in my life and I will again.

○ I have a right to think differently and believe in different things than other people.

○ I have got interesting ideas and experiences that I can share if I want to.

○ Making mistakes is OK – I can learn from these – and it allows others to as well.

○ I can understand and forgive other people who have hurt me, being 'adult' means that I can start to sort things out for myself; I don't have to go on blaming people.

○ Sometimes new experiences are very exciting.

○ I have inner creative talents which need a chance to grow.

○ The 'perfect' teacher does not exist – the 'good enough' one does!

○ I do not need everyone's approval all the time to know that I'm trying my hardest.

○ Unless I create some time and treats for myself, I will not have the energy to support a self-esteem and positive behaviour policy.

Now select one that you need to believe in more strongly and write it down where you can see it every day – read it and believe it!

LANGUAGE, SELF-ESTEEM AND BEHAVIOUR

CTS

Aim To help staff consider that how they talk to children can affect their whole lives. To help staff understand the impact of negative and positive statements and to realise that being positive is often more time-consuming and requires a lot of patience and self-discipline.

Pairs In pairs, participants are asked to each remember back to school days where they felt humiliated or hurt by the way in which a teacher responded to them. Discuss this with their partner.

Reporting back The group discusses the significance of language in terms of how it can effect the self-esteem of individuals.

Handout 1 Each participant is given Handout 1 to read through.

Discussion The facilitator asks participants to consider how often they use Example A language as opposed to Example B language, and why this is so. For example it is often quicker and easier, Example B language requires more thought and patience and is therefore more time-consuming.

Handout 2 Each participant is given Handout 2, **Stereotyping or accurate description?** and asked to categorise each statement as either stereotyping or accurate description.

Discussion The facilitator initiates discussion on the importance of ensuring that statements about children are accurate descriptions about specific incidents and therefore do not become generalised 'truisms' about a child's behaviour. Discuss how this language standard could be incorporated into a behaviour policy.

Action Plan Read and take away Handout 3, **Guidelines on how to enhance children's self-esteem through the positive use of language.**

It is often difficult when we are stressed or annoyed not to criticise a child, but it is possible to achieve the effect that we desire in a more positive way.

Example A	Example B
"Well John you've made a total mess of it as usual!"	"You haven't quite understood this section here John, bring your book out and I'll go through it with you."
"What do you think you're doing Matthew?"	"Matthew, it's time you put that book away and started work on your history project."
"Why don't you ever listen when I tell you what to do Sarah?"	"You have to fold the paper in half before you begin Sarah."
"Who told you to get that book?"	"You must wait until lunchtime if you wish to choose a new library book."
"Don't draw it like that!"	"Mary come and join the rest of the class now, please."
"Get out of the cupboard Mary, you stupid girl!"	"I think that you would find it easier drawing in pencil."

Ian Gyllenspetz

I keep telling you how lazy you are – why don't you change?

Stereotyping or accurate description?

Guidelines on how to enhance children's self-esteem through the positive use of language

○ Of course we are all going to 'blow our tops' and shout occasionally, but we only earn the right to shout if we regularly 'blast' the children with praise!

○ Be positive and generous with praise. Remember to thank children for something done well.

○ Consider the way in which you offer criticism and focus on a positive target for improvement, rather than emphasising what is negative e.g. "When you pushed Jenny off her chair that was a very dangerous thing to do", not "You are a nasty little bully." Don't use sarcasm, or 'put downs' and remember an unkind word is remembered far longer than a kind one.

○ Look for opportunities to praise a 'naughty' child. Don't call children by nick-names.

○ Don't put labels on a child e.g. bully, stupid, naughty, etc. Label the behaviour instead.

○ A quiet reminder can often prevent any further trouble.

○ Don't interrupt children when they are speaking. Listen carefully to pick up on unspoken clues as to what they are really trying to tell you.

○ Give warm body language, smile and create a friendly atmosphere.

○ Don't mix praise with criticism e.g. "That is a neat piece of work but you'll really have to work on your spellings" – the child will only remember the criticism.

○ Ask any questions gently; don't appear too prying. Give positive and active attention when you are listening, don't fidget around or look distracted. Speak to the children in a polite and courteous manner.

○ Say sorry if you have made a mistake, been unfair or given an unclear explanation – don't be afraid to apologise.

Aim   To help teachers share problems, to distance themselves from any negative pattern they may have become trapped in and to re-examine the inner worlds of the children who are causing them anxiety.

Method   Regular Circle-Time staff meetings are set aside for individual teachers to focus on individual children from their own class who are causing them anxiety.

Round   Members of staff are asked to describe how they feel when they are with the children whose behaviour worries them. Typical responses include: feelings of failure, anger, inadequacy, despair, anxiety or sadness. It is often useful if the facilitator volunteers to be the first person to speak as initially this task can appear threatening.

Question   Have we become trapped in any negative patterns of behaviour with these children which is preventing us from understanding them?

Typical answers include "I always seem to be looking for fault with her."
"As soon as I hear this whiney voice I feel irritated."
"I find I can no longer be bothered with him because he always rejects my encouragement or praise."

Discussion   A teacher presents a brief outline of the problem s/he is concerned about. An open discussion then follows on understanding the inner world of that particular pupil through the 'Maslow' model page 59, taking into account factors at home and school which may be destructively affecting the child's world.

Reflection   What does the child's behaviour tell/ask us?

Brainstorm   Anything that could be offered to motivate the child to change or break the pattern of his/her behaviour, e.g. one to one time with someone, giving the child an opportunity to help a younger child etc.

Action Plan   Enlist the practical support from other members of staff that the teacher needs in order to "survive'. Work out an Action Plan building in a special time for the teacher and child to talk together.

Round   Session ends with the same teacher focusing on another child s/he has to nominate who has shown improvement, describing what progress has been made and how s/he has contributed to this progress – we must take time to learn from our successes.

PARENTAL SUPPORT FOR THE
SELF-ESTEEM AND BEHAVIOUR POLICY

Aim   To help staff understand and appreciate the benefits of working with parents to achieve shared aims.

Pairs   Can you remember what your parents did that made you feel either really good or really bad about yourself? Feedback to circle.

Discussion   Is it possible to have an effective self-esteem policy if we have not truly involved the parents?

Question   What pressures are parents under that can lower their self-esteem?

Round   Facilitator asks those teachers who are also parents to share anything they feel guilty about, where their children are concerned. Teachers who are not parents can contribute any concerns that they have been told by parents.

Handout   **Case study of single parent and naughty child.**

Discussion   How could this parent have been helped and involved more by the school?

Action Plan   What can we do to involve parents more in our school and enlist their support in our self-esteem and behaviour policy?

Case study of single parent and naughty child

Gavin was late again for school. I can't get him to bed at night so he's always tired and terrible to wake up in the morning. He's lost that new football shirt I bought him, so he'll be in trouble again at P.E. He says it's been stolen but I'm not going up to the school. I feel the teachers look down on me because I'm not married and because I can't always afford the right equipment for school – they should try and manage on £80 a week for everything.

I did try going up to the school to meet Gavin's new teacher, I thought I'd really make an effort this year, but I felt she was judging me and Gavin, and didn't try to understand how hard it is at home.

Gavin gets into trouble because he doesn't do his work properly. I can't help him because I'm not brainy enough. He says that the teachers think he's just lazy, but he can't do the work and they don't take enough time to help him. I'm not going up to the school about it though, what's the point? They don't want to listen and they don't like people like us. I don't blame Gavin for hating school. I do want him to get on and make something of himself, but I don't think I'd like going to a place like that myself. I like Mrs Watts, the dinner lady, she looks out for Gavin at lunchtimes and talks to him. He likes her best at school, he thinks she's the only person there that cares about him.

I don't go to parent's evenings any more, I'm too embarrassed. All the other parents hear good things about their kids, but when it's my turn the teacher just moans about Gavin's behaviour. It's funny how they never say how good he is with younger kids or that he knows just about everything there is to know about football. That takes just as much brains as learning tables.

Section 3

**Circle-Time Sessions for developing
a lunchtime policy**

SUPPORTING AND DEVELOPING
A LUNCHTIME POLICY

Are you aware of any of the following problems occurring in your school during the lunchtime period?	✓ or ✗
Bad behaviour, e.g. lots of kicking or spoiling of each other's games.	
Children complaining they are bored.	
Bullying from individual children to other children – ranging from verbal threat to physical fight, formation of 'gangs' leading to conflict and exclusion of certain children who are told they are not allowed to join in, victimisation of a particular child.	
Tale-telling after lunchtimes.	
Children standing against the wall.	
Queues outside the headteacher's office.	
Frequent grumblings from lunchtime supervisors.	
Lunchtime supervisors frequently shouting at children.	
General apathy amongst lunchtime supervisors about playing games with children in the playground.	
Lunchtime supervisors feeling resentful because of inconsistencies between playtime and lunchtime standards of behaviour.	
Wet playtimes being barely manageable for the lunchtime supervisors.	
Occasional complaints from parents.	

The only way forward is to work together with the Lunchtime Supervisors.

SUPPORTING AND DEVELOPING A LUNCHTIME POLICY

Aim To help teachers focus on lunchtimes and the importance of overcoming negative attitudes in order to begin to view lunchtimes as part of the 'whole' school experience they offer children.

Round What is making you, the teacher, fed-up about lunchtimes at the moment? Typical answers include:- children telling tales during and after lunchtime, lunchtime supervisors complaining about the same naughty children everyday.

Handout 1 **A lunchtime supervisor's point of view.**

Handout 2 **What the supervisors say.**

Questions Are the points raised in the handouts typical of your school? How do you think the lunchtime supervisors in your school feel about their roles? Are you aware of the views and feelings of the lunchtime supervisors? Do you have regular contact with all the lunchtime supervisors?

Handout 3 **Questions that the Maslow Hierarchy raises.** Remember from Maslow's hierarchy of needs that unmet needs lead to low self-esteem which, in turn, leads to negative ways of relating to people. If you want lunchtime supervisors to develop more positive relationships you will have to raise their self-esteem. (It is also important to talk to catering staff about issues of self-esteem, so that they too greet children and serve them with respect).

Brainstorm Ask for any ideas to help lunchtime supervisors and improve lunchtimes.

Follow Up Perhaps you need an INSET day to work through all the systems the school could create to help lunchtime supervisors create happier lunchtimes.

A lunchtime supervisor's point of view

Lunchtimes are always a rush, there never seems enough time and I have to nag the kids to hurry. Some of them never finish all their food.

It's really hard when a child does something wrong. They can be very rude and if you tell them something, they don't take much notice. I told Alice off yesterday and she said her mum had told her not to bother about anything I say, as I'm only a dinner lady.

Sometimes I stand one of the children against the wall, but it doesn't do much good. They often think it's a laugh and enjoy the attention.

It gets so bad sometimes, that I shout at them and I really hate doing that, but I just don't know what else I can do. If you send a child to the head you don't know if it does any good because you never hear anything back, and anyway I don't really want the kids to get into serious trouble, so I put up with things I wouldn't normally put up with from my own children.

It's just as bad if they do something good, because you can only say well done and it's not really enough to make them feel special. If children help you, they like it to be noticed by the others, so I would like to have some sort of badge for them to wear.

Sometimes the children are really horrid to each other; they say rude things about the food so that the others won't eat it. It really worries me if they go without their lunch.

I have tried talking to the teachers about problems, but most of them are so busy they don't want me bothering them. The awful thing is that I just seem to nag about the naughty ones.

The lunchtime supervisors often get niggly with each other because everything is so chaotic and there's a lot of backstabbing.

It's a nightmare in the playground. Rehana got hit in the face with the football today and had a terrible nose bleed. I get mad when the boys aren't careful, but what can you expect? They don't have enough room to play somewhere safe.

There always seem to be children who are bored with nothing to do, so they just go round spoiling everybody else's games. I did look in the shed to see if there was any equipment to use in the playground, but it all seems to have been lost or ended up on the school roof.I found a good washing line and got a group playing a skipping game, but then John kept running up and stopping the rope, so in the end I had to put it away.

The boys have got a craze on American wrestling at the moment. Everyday someone gets hurts. I try to stop them, but they just move away where I can't see them and start again. They feel resentful that I'm spoiling their fun.

We aren't given any guidance or back-up from the staff. I'd like some ideas of what to do with the children to keep them occupied. I want to be more involved, not just a minder, but I don't know what to do.

The end of lunchtimes are just as chaotic. There doesn't seem to be any proper system so there's lots of pushing and shouting. It's bedlam. The children go screaming into the school, it can't be a very good way to start afternoon lessons.

What the supervisors say

Questions that the Maslow hierarchy raises

○ Are the children physically and emotionally safe at school?

○ Do lunchtime supervisors have the use of effective incentives and sanctions in order to uphold their status and authority?

○ Do lunchtime supervisors share a sense of 'belonging' to the school?

○ What is the status of lunchtime supervisors within the school?

○ Are they involved in assemblies or given regular positive feedback from the head and teachers?

○ Are they seen as valued members of the school community?

○ What help is given to lunchtime supervisors to encourage them to be creative, play games and build relationships with the children?

○ Are there adequate play facilities and equipment?

RAISING THE SELF-ESTEEM OF LUNCHTIME SUPERVISORS

Once teachers have held a Circle-Time Session for themselves to focus on lunchtimes it becomes clear that the first responsibility for the school is to raise the self-esteem of the supervisors so that they feel valued, respected and more able to take on the challenge of changing systems and changing their own behaviour.

Next the school needs to hold Circle-Time Sessions with their supervisors just to listen to their concerns and anxieties. There are always considerable resentments and grumbles, but it is important at this stage just to listen sympathetically to them in a non-defensive way. Subsequent Circle-Time Sessions can then be structured to focus on various options for developing new incentives and a sanctions policy. These options can be tried out and their varying degrees of success reported back during the Circle-Time Sessions. It is best to hold one hourly or half hourly Circle-Time Session just before for just after a lunchtime duty. Some schools rely on the goodwill of their supervisors. Some pay for the hour out of school funds.

It is important that any new system incorporates a whole school focus on raising the status of lunchtime supervisors so that children and parents do not see them as 'second-class citizens'. Many children already have the view because they never actually physically see lunchtime supervisors as part of the school staff. The children experience their teachers as the powerful ones as they have dominant profiles around the school, holding all the incentives, sanctions and resources. Lunchtime supervisors on the other hand often have low profiles, inferior or no incentives and sanctions, and no access to outside resources.

The first major task, therefore, is to raise the profile of lunchtime supervisors and enhance their status. This can be done by:-

❍ holding meetings with them

❍ drawing up Golden Rules with them to govern behaviour in the dining hall and playground

❍ drawing up Golden Rules for safety in the playground – these rules must also be adhered to by all members of staff at playtime as well as lunchtime

❍ devising effective incentives and sanctions that can be used by each supervisor

○ holding assemblies which focus on lunchtimes and Golden Rules to which supervisors are invited

○ inviting supervisors to attend class Circle-Time Sessions

○ allotting each supervisor one or two specific classes and creating time for the supervisor to spend with the teachers to discuss the progress of the children

○ encouraging teachers to explain the importance of the supervisor's role to children, during class time and through the curriculum.

○ providing a section in the school prospectus about lunchtimes, introducing the supervisors and commenting on their important contribution to school life

○ providing INSET courses that teach first aid and the developmental needs of children

○ rehearsing the fire drill at lunchtimes so that everyone feels safe about procedures

○ ensuring that supervisors are informed of day-to-day events, e.g. if a child has permission to remain in school during lunchtime

○ organise formal 'handovers' between lunchtime supervisors and teachers where supervisors can hand over the names of any children due for rewards or sanctions.

What midday supervisors resolved to do after they had been involved in Circle-Time Sessions.

> I have learned to be a better listener
>
> I am better prepared to deal with a crisis
>
> I will give children more of me
>
> I have a better understanding of children's needs
>
> It has made me more aware of my faults

GUIDELINES FOR LUNCHTIME SUPERVISORS

Aim   To focus on guidelines for good relationships and to draw up some Golden Rules with lunchtime supervisors.

Handout 1   **Guidelines for good relationships.**

Pairs   In pairs, the participants are given two or three items from the handout (depending on number of participants) to discuss and report back on.

Questions   1. Do you agree with the guidelines on the handout?

2. What ideas do we want to adopt as guidelines to help us make lunchtimes happier?

Handout 2   **Golden Rules for lunchtime supervisors.**

Action Plan   Draw up a list of Golden Rules for ourselves referring to handout 2, **Golden Rules** drawn up by Kilmington School's lunchtime supervisors during a Circle-Time Session.

PLEASE NOTE:

If good relationships have already been developed by the lunchtime supervisors this session may be the right time to ask each person, after they have discussed the guidelines, to identify one strength they already possess and something they need to work on.

Examples of a self-assessment list from Dunston School's lunchtime supervisors.

I'm good at building relationships, but I need to listen more

I can chat easily with the children, but I'm not so good about giving out stickers

I'm good at playing with the children, but I'd like to know more games

I get on well with the children, but I need to keep my voice low

I'm good at listening to the children, but not so good at chatting to them

I'm better at talking to the teachers about children's problems, but I'd like to be able to mix more easily with the children

Guidelines for good relationships

❍ *TREAT ALL CHILDREN FAIRLY AND EQUALLY*
It is all too easy to jump to wrong conclusions about a situation. The children must be given an opportunity to explain their behaviour. Don't act on hearsay; only act on what you are sure you saw.

❍ *BE FRIENDLY AND APPROACHABLE*
Children need to see you as someone who is approachable and ready to listen to them. A cold or distant manner will stop them from approaching you.

❍ *GIVE GENTLE REMINDERS*
Children often simply forget some rules e.g. running in the corridor. A gentle reminder is often all that is needed to correct this.

❍ *STAY CALM*
Try to stay calm at all times. This will help you to remain in authority and be effective.

❍ *SMILE*
Try and remember to smile at the children, they will then see you as someone warm and friendly.

❍ *TRY AND CHAT*
Be willing to chat to the children about their news, interests and activities.

❍ *GIVE PRAISE*
Praise is more effective than criticism so try and use praise frequently.

❍ *GIVE INCENTIVES*
Ask the school if there are any special stickers or incentives that you could use.

❍ *BE FAIR*
Be fair with punishment system – if you didn't spot the trouble don't rely on the word of other children – take time to talk it through but look out for it deliberately.

❍ *BE POLITE*
Set a good example to the children by speaking politely to them. Ask girls as well as boys to do the heavy jobs.

○ *AVOID GETTING INTO A CONFRONTATION*
Don't argue with a child, this undermines your authority. Repeat your request calmly, then use your sanctions system.

○ *HELP A CHILD 'BACK OUT' OF AN AWKWARD SITUATION*
If a child is deliberately rude ask them to repeat what they said. This allows the child to retract the statement or apologise. Accept any apology graciously and don't continue to scold.

○ *DON'T SHOUT*
Avoid shouting at all times. If the noise level is high ask the school if there are other ways you can gain silence. Don't shout in anger.

○ *DON'T USE SARCASM.*
Don't belittle children by using sarcasm – this leads to resentment.

○ *DON'T USE LABELS*
Don't give children negative labels such as, 'naughty", 'rude', or 'stupid'. Tell the child their behaviour is unacceptable, but remember labels 'stick'.

○ *WATCH OUT FOR LONERS*
Watch out for lonely or isolated children. Talk to them and try and involve them in games with the other children.

These Golden Rules were drawn up during a Circle-Time Session by the lunchtime supervisors of Kilmington School.

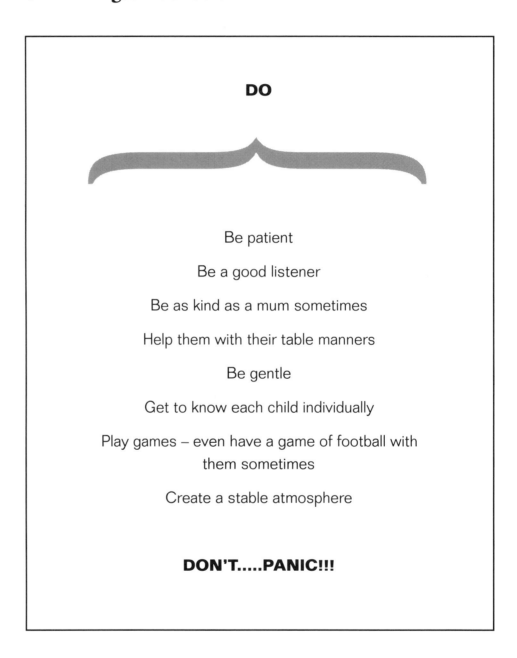

DO

Be patient

Be a good listener

Be as kind as a mum sometimes

Help them with their table manners

Be gentle

Get to know each child individually

Play games – even have a game of football with them sometimes

Create a stable atmosphere

DON'T.....PANIC!!!

INCENTIVES FOR LUNCHTIME SUPERVISORS – SOME IDEAS

> The lunchtime staff are now able to reward positive behaviour and they join us for any relevant assemblies. This area of work has more than justified time spent on it as behaviour at lunchtimes has improved and the lunchtime supervisors now feel much more valued within the school and the teaching staff see them as valued members of the whole team.
>
> *Headteacher's report Woodlands School, Salisbury.*

Special stickers:

Commending aspects of behaviour e.g. good table manners, kindness, being helpful, these can be given to the children by the supervisor.

Lunchtime helper badges

These badges can be given out for various responsibilities decided upon by the supervisors and could include

- wiping tables
- being in charge of equipment
- supervising the quiet area
- organising games
- teaching games to younger children
- litter duty
- helping lonely children.

These can be given out on a daily/weekly basis to all children wherever possible, in a non-discriminatory way, i.e. both girls and boys can lift and move items of furniture.

Table of the week

A special table is attractively set up with a table cloth, vase of flowers etc. and on a weekly basis is used as a privilege for any 'table' which has behaved well. If one particular child persistently spoils the efforts of his/her table to gain access to 'Table of the Week' the remaining children can be given the privilege whilst the 'offender' remains at an ordinary table.

Display area

Create an eye-catching display area in the dining hall on which the lunchtime supervisors put up their *Golden Stars of The Week* i.e. a list of names of children they have commended that week.

Positive booklets

There are two different systems that can be used by the supervisors.

SYSTEM 1
The supervisors have a booklet of blank pages on which they write the name of any child they wish to commend for good behaviour. The supervisor hands it to the teacher with a positive comment. The child takes the page to his/her teacher and is rewarded with a sticker, star or any other agreed incentive.

SYSTEM 2.
The supervisors have a booklet of pages on which are printed a variety of commendable behaviours.

I AM PLEASED WITH YOU BECAUSE YOU:-

refused to be drawn into a fight

have been helpful

showed good manners

played well with other children

queued patiently

asked someone to join in a game

NAME..

SUPERVISOR...

TEACHER...

The appropriate behaviour is ticked and the page signed by the supervisors and the child's teacher. These pages can then be taken home to show the parents.

A special lunchtime certificate

A certificate praising positive behaviour is issued to all those children who did not receive any 'bad behaviour' notes during the course of a term. These can be given out by the lunchtime supervisors during a special school assembly.

Dinner Ladies Special Certificate

Well done for good behaviour at lunchtimes.

Developing sanctions

It is important that schools develop sanctions systems that can be used equally by the teachers and the supervisors. The Privilege-Time system is very effective in this way.

All children should receive one warning before any sanction is applied. Some persistent offenders may treat warnings as a 'free kick' so they may lose their right to them and each supervisor must use her discretion when to remove the privilege of one warning.

System 1. The supervisors have a booklet of blank pages. As an official warning, the name of any child who breaks a Golden Rule is entered into the booklet. If the child manages not to break another rule they can watch their name being crossed out at the end of the playtime. If the child repeats his/her action or breaks another Golden Rule during the lunchtime the supervisor hands the page to the child's teacher, who enforces the agreed sanction, e.g. the loss of Privilege-Time.

System 2. The supervisors have a booklet of printed statements about behaviour. The appropriate behaviour is ticked and if the child repeats the behaviour the page is handed to the child's teacher to enforce agreed sanctions e.g. loss of Privilege-Time.

EXAMPLE

I AM DISAPPOINTED IN YOU BECAUSE YOU DELIBERATELY:-

called unkind names

ignored an instruction

physically hurt another child

were rude to an adult

were inconsiderate in your behaviour

threw stones

NAME..

SUPERVISOR..

TEACHER..

To avoid the label 'naughty' being attached to any child, it is important that the supervisor tries to redress the balance by finding one commendable aspect of a child's behaviour, if s/he has received a 'disappointed' note, during the following two week period. This might mean using some active form of encouragement such as the giving of a responsibility which the child can succeed at and earn a commendation.

Children 'beyond' lunchtime incentives and sanctions

For any child who proves to be 'beyond' this incentives and sanction system, the next stage is the use of a personal contract, which targets specific behavioural goals, between the child, supervisor and teacher. If this is still not effective, the child's parents must be included to endorse the contract with the understanding that if the child fails to reach his/her targets, s/he may lose the privilege of attending school lunchtimes.

THE DINING HALL

Ongoing Circle-Time Sessions are needed with the lunchtime supervisors to identify areas of concern and systems that are not working effectively.

Typical issues raised during these meeting are:

❍ high noise levels

❍ pushing in queues

❍ children being put off their food by remarks from other children about the food or poor table manners

❍ insufficient time causing meals to be 'rushed'

❍ having to rush slow eaters

It is important to establish an orderly and quiet entry into the dining hall. Younger or more timid children can find the noise and jostling intimidating, consequently lunchtimes become a frightening experience for them. One group of lunchtime supervisors, at Christ the King School, solved this problem through playing assembly type tapes of music. Some schools twin classes of older and younger children together, so that each child will look after the younger child during queuing and if necessary, help cut up food, help put away dining utensils, stack chairs etc.

The lunchtime supervisors must have an effective system to reduce noise levels when it is required, the 'hand up' system is very effective. The supervisor raises her hand and all the children follow suit, at the same time remaining silent. (Younger children can place a finger on their lips). This system works well if it is also used by the teachers. Supervisors can also use the 'hand up' system when giving out rewards such as table of the week, to provide a further incentive for achieving quiet.

The issue of 'good table manners' should be addressed and discussed with children. As mentioned in the checklist (page 109), one effective way of dealing with this is through drama and also by encouraging the children to itemise unacceptable table manners and discussing why they are unacceptable. This is important for those children who do not receive any formal training in table manners at home and therefore might not perceive their behaviour as unacceptable.

Family grouping is another useful and effective way of improving table manners. Each child has a turn at being the 'head of the family' and responsible for correcting unacceptable table manners. The other children must be willing to amend their behaviour and act appropriately. A problem for table 'monitors' or heads of the table are those children who are 'slow eaters'. It is best, therefore, to have a complete table of slow-eaters who have very patient kind monitors who are prepared to give them more time.

To minimise time spent collecting food, some schools provide each child with a 'plane tray' which contains both courses. Alternatively, the supervisors can wheel a trolley round dispensing the second course and avoid time wasted in queuing.

Entering and leaving the dining hall can be equally chaotic and noisy so orderly systems should be in operation. Some schools have also introduced the same calming music they use in assembly at lunchtimes. Allowing one table to exit at a time is effective and can be determined in various ways, whether on a rota system, or for good behaviour, or the first table to achieve silence etc. Also Studley Green School devised a large card system for the two sittings. Each table has a large card with the names of the children on that table printed on it. The names of children in the first sitting are on one side, and the names of those in the second sitting are on the reverse. When the first sitting table has finished the table monitor takes out the large card and hands it to the second sitting table monitor who gathers together all the children on her table and proceeds into the hall without having to queue.

Wet lunchtimes

Wet lunchtimes can be a nightmare for teachers and lunchtime supervisors if there are inadequate facilities to occupy the children's time.
Each class should have a box containing games, scrap paper, activity books, etc. Lunchtime supervisors could have groups of children to play circle games with, or one supervisor could take a group of children to the library for a story.

Schools can also designate certain special activities, drama, games, model making etc. just for wet play-times so that children are compensated for and do not feel so disappointed at losing the opportunity to play outside. In this way, such times can be made more enjoyable for staff and children rather than nerve-wracking or boring periods to be endured.

Top juniors chosen for the special privilege of wearing a Lunchtime Helper badge can go to other younger classes to help them to play games.

HOW TO HELP CHILDREN PLAY
IN THE PLAYGROUND

Circle-Time Sessions can be used to draw up a structured lunchtime policy taking into account all aspects of playground time i.e. play areas, procedures, facilities and equipment which could be made available to lunchtime supervisors to use.

Encouraging playground games

If focus is given to playground games during P.E. lessons or topic lessons the benefits can be seen in the playground, as this both raises the status of lunchtime supervisors and initiates ideas which motivate the children to play on their own. One school focused on skipping for a week. The children were shown a video and a 'skipathon' was held. This encouraged all the children, both boys and girls to become involved in skipping games in the playground. Another tested idea is to invite outsiders with particular skills, such as jugglers into the school to teach the children how to do it.

P.E. lessons should, ideally, focus on playground games once every half-term. It is also a useful policy to elect older children who will initiate and demonstrate playground games to the younger children. Such children can be given an 'I'm a good friend' badge. Teachers or supervisors must check they know some good games, and can teach them without being bossy.

Playground equipment

Many schools say that they have attempted to provide equipment for use in the playground, but that it is soon lost or broken. To overcome this problem it is advisable to introduce one piece of equipment at a time, which can be focused upon during an assembly. 'Lunchtime Helpers' can be elected from the children and given a notebook – itemising all pieces of equipment. Borrowers must have their initials singed by the 'helpers' beside the equipment they have taken, and these are only deleted when the equipment is returned and its condition checked. Also, whilst the piece of equipment may be used with other children, it is the borrowers responsibility and s/he must not allow another group of children to take it over.

Suggested equipment for the playground

Balls of various types and sizes, plastic hoops, bean bags, long washing lines for skipping, elastic for 'French skipping', Scratch (hand-velcro bats and soft balls), skittles, various shaped blocks of wood sanded down, large lego.

It is crucial that teachers also make time in their P.E. lessons to teach the children the games that use these small pieces of equipment. Small balls are often put into the equipment but not many children know what games to play with them.

Marked games

A line-painting machine can be rented to outline various games such as hopscotch onto the playground surface. Children can be encouraged to design their own games as well.

Outdoor dressing up box

A box containing items of clothing and accessories to be worn over the children's own clothes e.g. hats, gloves, coats, shawls, bags, waistcoats. (Net curtains are also very popular!)

Quiet area

A designated area is marked off to be used as a quiet area. Seats can be arranged in the area or carpet tiles put down each day. This area is specifically for reading, board games, activity books etc., which can be provided in a box. Two quiet area helpers ensure that the equipment is returned to the box and that the area is only used for quiet pursuits i.e. no running, shouting, fighting.

Football policy

It is perhaps important with regard to football playing to ask the question "What are some children learning about our school values?" Do the 'football squad' in your school mostly consist of older, stronger and more dominant boys, and are the younger, weaker children or the girls excluded? Does football dominate most of the play area and are other children and adults frequently hurt by the ball?

If a handful of boys are allowed to dominate with the football, the hidden message to the children is that when resources are limited (i.e. small playground space, no equipment) they are given to the strongest and largest males. This results in bad gender learning and certainly contravenes any equal opportunities policy. Some schools avoid tackling this problem because of worries that these older boys, if deprived of their football, will engage in anti-social activities such as forming gangs to bully other children. A sound football policy is therefore essential to reflect the caring values promoted in a whole school policy on self-esteem and positive behaviour.

All children who wish to play football should attend a large meeting once a term with teachers and lunchtime supervisors. Excessive numbers may mean that a rota system has to be used and if playground space is limited and there is no special area designated for football, a daily time-limit can be imposed to allow other children opportunity to use the space as well.

Golden Rules are drawn up to govern acceptable behaviour and any child who violates a Golden Rule may lose the privilege of playing football for a set period of time. Some schools elect 'captains' to be responsible for choosing teams. The captains (both boys and girls) are elected on their ability to follow certain criteria when choosing teams. They must include people with good skills, people who need to improve their skills, people who allow themselves and other to make mistakes, both girls and boys.

The football policy should include equal opportunities for both boys and girls and in fact, this equality of opportunity should be in force in all games e.g. netball and be promoted during P.E. lessons as well.

We are very limited in playground space, but found that if we stopped the older boys playing football in the main part of the playground they became disruptive to the younger children's games elsewhere. The younger children and older girls tend to play in groups, fairly small groups, but nothing was recognisable as a game apart from chasing other groups.

We felt they needed something to enhance their play, the first things that came to mind were dressing-up clothes, but not very practical for damp playgrounds in winter. Then we thought about hats and bags, this meant going to all the local jumble sales and asking around parents etc. We ended up with quite a large box of assorted hats, but could still do with a policeman's helmet, a taxi driver's cap, and some large, pretty ladies hats, and a better selection of bags, scarves are also a possibility as they can be washed easily. It's a good idea to put a child in charge of collecting them at the end of break.

At the moment we are making up cards with printed instructions for skipping, ball, marble, jacks and pencil and paper games. For this you need a quiet area in the playground and for the skipping the dinner ladies help turn the rope and read out the rhymes for the children to learn. All these are kept in cardboard boxes and the children fetch them at dinner time and collect them when the bell goes.

We were given a small selection of large cars and lorries, the infant boys love them, but they do not last long, and cause a few sharing problems.

A report written by the Senior Lunchtime Supervisor from Potterne Primary School

Now the play areas sound like a happy seaside sound...happy playing sounds.

Shepherd Spring Infant School

Playtime can seem a long time to a young child if there is nothing to do or no-one to play with. At the moment the playground offers little. Some children get bored with little to occupy or stimulate them for up to 30 minutes and it is not surprising that this can lead to arguments, kicking and fighting or to children being isolated with no-one to play with.

Lunchtime supervisors can help by organising a variety of games for children to play. It does not need a large group of children to start a game. When children see that you value games and enjoy playing them they soon join in. Choose a game that you know well and feel confident to start with. Ask 1 or 2 children to join with you and start playing. Show you are enjoying the game and give praise to the players. As other children stop to watch the game invite them to join in the fun. Do not let anyone spoil the game and make sure it does not last too long.

Tips when playing games.

1. Choose games you know and the children know to begin with.

2. Try to get a mixture of boys and girls, older and younger children.

3. Start with a few children and encourage others to join in.

4. Keep it short – rather play 2 short games than 1 long one and the children lose interest.

5. Children who try to spoil the game should be excluded for that game, but let everyone join in the next time.

Playground policy from Margaret Stancombe School

CIRCLE-GAMES FOR THE PLAYGROUND

I sent a letter

In a circle, facing inwards, one child walks around the outside of the circle saying "I sent a letter to my friend and on the way I dropped it. Someone must have picked it up and put in their pocket. It wasn't you, it wasn't you, it was you ." At this point the child taps another child on the shoulder, who must chase him/her around the circle. If the child is 'caught' s/he becomes part of the circle and the 'catcher' becomes the letter sender, otherwise the first child repeats the process.

Cat and mice

In a circle facing inwards, five children are chosen, four become mice and stand in the centre of the circle, the fifth becomes a cat and stands outside the circle. When the supervisor says 'go', the cat enters the circle and tries to tag the mice. The mice must remain inside the circle and stand still once they are tagged. The last mouse to be touched then becomes the cat and four new mice are chosen.

The giant's dinner

In a circle facing inwards, one child is chosen to be the giant, is blindfolded and stands in the centre of the circle. Near the giant, an object is placed on the floor to represent the giant's dinner. The supervisor selects a child who has to creep into the circle and try and steal the giant's dinner. If the giant hears the intruder s/he says "I hear someone in my castle, There!" and points to where s/he thinks the intruder is. If the giant is correct the intruder returns to their place in the circle and another child is chosen. If the intruder successfully steals the giant's dinner and returns to their place in the circle then s/he becomes the giant.

The pirate's treasure

In a circle facing inwards. In the centre, treasure, (a football), is placed on an island (inside a hoop) guarded by a chosen pirate. Children can run into the circle and try and capture the treasure. Any child who succeeds in capturing the treasure and returning to their place in the circle becomes the new pirate. The pirate can tag any intruders before they reach their place even if they have the treasure, and they are then out of the game. The supervisor can also choose a new pirate.

Birds on the trees

In a circle children form groups of three. Two of the group are trees and face each other holding hands. The third child is the bird and stands in between the two trees. In the centre of the circle stands a lone bird. When the centre bird cries "fly" the trees arise their arms to allow each bird to change trees. At the same time, the centre bird tries to find a tree to lodge in. Once a tree has a new bird the children forming the tree drop their arms. The bird who is left without a tree goes into the centre. Children should remain on the inside of the circle during the change-over.

Cars

In a circle, children run in a clockwise direction on the signal 'go' pretending they are cars. They may overtake other cars, but not change direction. At the signal 'stop' all cars must halt, be silent and look at the supervisor. Those failing to do so or who bump into other cars must 'go into the garage for repairs' and miss a turn.

Circle ball

Children form small circles (limit numbers to six or seven) with one child standing in the centre holding a ball. This child throws or bounces the ball to each child in turn around the circle, who returns it to the centre. If a child in the circle fails to catch the ball s/he must go down on one knee. A second failure means going down on both knees and a third means taking the place of the child in the centre.

Name ball

In small circles with one child in the centre. This child throws the ball in the air and calls out the name of one of the players. That child must try to catch the ball, before it bounces more than once. If s/he is successful s/he takes the place of the child in the centre.

EMILY

Roll the ball

Children sit cross-legged in a circle. Two to four balls are rolled across the circle between players. The balls must not be thrown or bounced. The object of the game is to succeed in rolling a ball past a player and out of the circle; this scores one point. The ball is retrieved by the player who scores the point.

Skittle ball

In circles with a skittle in the centre, children take turns to throw a ball and try and knock the skittle over. If they are successful they score one point. The child who knocks the skittle over sets it back up. A variation can include a child in the centre trying to 'guard' the skittle.

Dodge ball

In a circle with one child in the centre. The children in the circle throw a ball and try to hit the child in the centre below the waist. The one who is successful takes their place. As a variation several can be in the centre.

Ball races

Children form two circles with a child in the centre of each. On the command "go" the child in the centre throws a ball to each player who in turn throws it back. Once each player has had their turn s/he crouches down. The first circle to have all players crouching down wins. Variations can be bouncing the ball or alternatively bouncing and throwing.

Chase the ball

In a circle with one player standing outside. The children in the circle pass or throw the ball to the next child around the circle. The single player has to try to run around the circle and reach their starting place before the ball does.

Circle relay

Children are divided into equal numbers and form two or more circles. On the command "go" each player in turn runs into the circle touches a beanbag in the centre and returns to their place and crouches down. The next player must not leave their place until the previous player has crouched down. The first circle to have all players crouching wins. A variation on the relay theme can be that each child in turn runs around the outside of his/her circle, returning to their place and crouching down.

Tell a good tale

End lunchtimes and begin classtime in a positive way with "Tell a good tale" circle. Children will often rush in to their teachers at the end of lunchtime to report a variety of injustices and complaints. The "Tell a good tale" circle is a brief ritual to avoid a tale-telling session and to establish a positive start to afternoon lessons. It also reinforces the ideal of positive behaviour.

During this short session children can only report good actions. A child nominates another child (not a best friend though) who has performed an act of kindness. The child is applauded or may even be nominated for a sticker in a few days time if their positive behaviour is noticed again.

WELL DONE, YOU DIDN'T CALL ME A NAME

CHECKLIST OF INITIATIVES THAT HELP CREATE HAPPIER LUNCHTIMES

		✓	✗
1	Do you have regular short meetings with your lunchtime supervisors to discuss current concerns? Do you invite your supervisors to any INSET days where you focus on promoting positive behaviour?		
2	Have you organised any INSET for the lunchtime supervisors on their chosen topics such as handling confrontations, understanding difficult children, initiating playground games, first aid?		
3	Do you invite your lunchtime supervisors to an assembly at the beginning of each new half-term to focus on expected standards of behaviour?		
4	Have your teachers and lunchtime supervisors sat down and worked out a) the physical safety rules? b) the 'Golden Rules' for behaviour?		
5	Have copies of these rules been typed up and distributed – and a covered copy put in the playground?		
6	In order to back up lunchtime supervisors do your teachers keep to exactly the same rules and procedures at playtime? If supervisors carry notebooks to write warnings – so should teachers, it gives them equal status.		
7	Have you given your lunchtime supervisors a list of children who are at risk healthwise?		
8	Have your gone through fire drill procedures at lunchtime with your supervisors?		
9	Do your staff fully appreciate the problems faced by lunchtime supervisors and do they back them up by the way they talk to and about the supervisors?		
10	Have you worked out any new incentives or sanctions with your supervisors (or is 'standing against the wall' still the only deterrent)?		

11	Have you made sure there is a daily handover or quick meeting time for your teacher and lunchtime supervisors to talk about the good and bad events affecting 'their' children?		
12	Have you tried teaming up a lunchtime supervisor to one or two classes on a termly basis so that they can build up closer and more understanding relationships with the teacher and pupils in that class?		
13	Have you ever given out 'Lunchtime Helpers' badges to your lunchtime supervisors so that they can give them to different children each day?		
14	Have you given your supervisors any stickers or certificates to reinforce the good behaviours already agreed on with them?		

The dining hall

		✓	✗
1	Are table manners discussed with the children either in assemblies or through the curriculum?		
2	Have you ever thought of turning your classroom (through drama) into a restaurant, where children dress up and take each other out for a 'posh' meal? (Miming eating wonderful dishes, but using real cutlery).		
3	Is your dining hall system working as best as it can or do you need to reconsider the queuing system?		
4	Have you ever given any system to your lunchtime supervisors to gain quiet during lunchtimes? e.g. clapping, whistle.		
5	Have you ever used the 'hand up' system to gain quiet?		
6	Have you ever suggested that supervisors could identify tables of well-mannered eaters who would earn the privilege of inviting special guests to their table?		
7	Do you have any incentives for children to encourage good behaviour and manners at the table? e.g. 'table of the week' – children sit at a special table with table cloth and flowers on it.		
8	Have you considered family grouping – allowing each child to enjoy the 'head of the family' role on a rota basis – signified by a special badge?		

Alleviating boredom (or preventing behaviour problems!)

		✓	✗
1	Do you have any equipment e.g. long washing lines (no handles) bean bags, elastic, wheelbarrow, soft balls, hoops, wooden blocks, heavy cardboard boxes, large lego available?		
2	Can children design their own games that can be marked in the playground either by themselves using chalk or painted on, e.g. hopscotch?		
3	Do teachers regularly help children to learn playground games and songs during P.E. lessons and other topic work?		
4	Do you have a book of simple playground games available for all staff use?		
5	Do you have an outdoor dressing-up box available for the younger children?		
6	Have you ever invited children from other classes to demonstrate games during lesson time?		
7	Have you debated the issue of football with children/supervisors/teachers? Have you ever considered setting a time for football, (15 minutes), football on 'rota' system, soft football?		
8	Do you have a 'quiet' area marked out (no running etc.) with old comics/blankets etc.? Do you limit the numbers using it at one time? If you can't have seats placed in it have you considered putting down carpet squares?		
9	Have you considered asking the P.T.A. for funds to help you to totally 'overhaul' your playground through proper playground 'landscaping'?		

Wet playtimes

		✓	✗
1	Has each teacher made and displayed a list of equipment children are allowed to use for wet playtimes?		
2	Does each class have an indoor games box for wet playtimes that is regularly replenished and reviewed?		
3	Have you considered using the video for films/cartoons on a class rota basis?		
4	Have you ever considered using the computer for games on a rota basis?		
5	Have you considered the possibility of an indoor option on cold playtimes?		
6	Have you considered giving older children responsibility badges so they can go in to other classes and teach other children games?		

Section 4

Circle-Time Sessions for use in the classroom

MAKING A SPACE FOR CIRCLE-TIME WITH PUPILS

Ideally all participants, including the teacher, should be seated on the same size chairs in their own classroom as opposed to the hall. I find even reception children think that meetings on chairs are more "grown up" and respond accordingly.

If the teacher does decide s/he'd rather they sit on the carpet then s/he must sit down with them.

Arrange your classroom or staffroom so that tables and bookshelves can be put back with the minimum of effort. Perhaps organise some older children wearing their 'teacher-helper' badges to do this task for you during a breaktime. Use the circle for a special half hour Circle-Time Session with a definite beginning and ending ritual– and then during the rest of the time till the next break, use the circle for teaching your other subjects. Many teachers report that a Circle-Time is particularly useful for music lessons, paired reading, P.S.E. and R.E. theories, story-time etc. When the next break arrives make sure that the 'teacher-helpers' arrive back to rearrange your class for you!

All children respond positively to continuous praise for "good listening bodies" as opposed to tellings off for "shuffling feet" – which only encourages more shuffles!

CIRCLE-TIME SESSIONS FOR CHILDREN – SOME GUIDELINES

○ All participants sit in a circle with the agreed leader. This could be the headteacher, a teacher, or anyone wishing to take this role. Some schools who regularly practise Circle-Time with children report that individual children soon learn to take it in turns to 'run' Circle-Sessions!

○ Initial Circle-Time Sessions can focus on the drawing up of Golden Rules for behaviour both within and outside the circle. Certain Golden Rules are absolute:

1 Do respect other people's rights to speak up and give opinions and don't use put downs.

2 Do ask for help with problems but don't blame anyone in the circle i.e. a child can ask for help to deal with being bullied, but he cannot name the bully in the circle. For example s/he must say "somebody has been pushing me" or "some people have left me out".

○ Circle-Time Sessions should occur on a regular basis, with all participants aware of when they will occur. They must not be pushed to one side when more 'important' things crop up as this gives the wrong message to participants.

○ The focus or themes of the session should take into account the current concerns/anxieties of the group.

○ Every session must include a positive focus. Either time should be given for participants to celebrate their own or another's success or the session can end with a decision to pursue a positive target. Time can be given at the end to join in a relaxed, co-operative, fun activity.

○ Adults or children may nominate themselves for help with a problem, but no-one can choose another person to focus in on.

○ All participants have a right to remain silent if they so choose, but must say 'pass' on their turn to speak in a 'round'. At the end of a round the person who started will ask those people who elected to pass if they now wish to make a contribution.

○ A 'talking' object should be used at least once during a Circle-Time Session. When a person holds a chosen object, e.g. a conch shell, s/he is allowed to speak. The object is passed around the circle allowing each participant the opportunity to put forward their views.

○ The ideal of confidentiality should be promoted, whilst accepting realistic constraints. For this reason children are warned to say as much as they feel is 'safe'. If they have anything they consider is too personal or controversial, which they need to discuss further, encourage them to ask for a 'special' chat later.

○ Be flexible. It is always helpful for the facilitator to take the time to prepare a simple programme of activities or a focus for Circle-Time, but as the facilitator becomes more experienced then they will become confident enough to go with the flow of ideas or concerns presented by the group.

○ Limit time spent on Circle-Time Sessions. 10 minutes for younger children, 20-30 minutes for older children, making it overlong will kill interest.

○ Vary activities by spending some time on games, rounds, discussions etc. Aim to make Circle-Time enjoyable.

○ Evaluate Circle-Time Sessions regularly (e.g. the most boring/the most interesting part for me was...)

○ Look out for the very withdrawn child who consistently says 'pass'. Prior to Circle-Time ask them to get an idea ready for a very non-threatening round e.g. "my favourite food". If they are still to timid perhaps they could present a picture instead, or whisper their statement to a puppet who speaks to the circle for them.

○ Make sure that you or the children follow up any injustices or things that are 'going wrong' for them. Circle work must not exist in isolation, it must be used as a vehicle to address problems and find acceptable solutions.

○ Circle-Time Sessions should allow time for children to reflect on any issues that concern them.

○ Designate a regular time, which all the children are aware of, when you will be available for a special chat. This time should be to discuss things, which can't be sorted out during Circle-Time Sessions, i.e. too private or controversial. Any child should know that they can ask.

○ Circle-Time should begin and end with certain enjoyable rituals chosen by the group. Some Circle-Time Sessions end with a positive round, or a fun game or a gentle, 'calming' time.

CIRCLE-TIME STRUCTURES

Games
These are used to unite the group. They provide enjoyment, break tensions, exert their own discipline and encourage self-control and group participation. They are useful for stimulating verbal and physical interaction. Many of the games can be adapted to introduce abstract concepts such as trust and co-operation.

Rounds using the conch strategy
Each group has a special 'talking' object e.g. a conch shell. A theme or idea is chosen as the focus for a round; sometimes a sentence is started which each participant must complete e.g. I feel happy when...... Each participant takes a turn to speak when s/he is holding the conch shell. Every comment is acceptable,participants may elect to 'pass' and no-one may comment on what anyone else has said. At the end the facilitator offers anybody who passed a second chance.

Pairwork
The facilitator divides the group into pairs (A & B) and provides a question or a theme. Each pair member reflects on, then talks to each other about the focus. Several minutes are allowed for this, and then each pair summarises their account for the group. At this stage, A can either recount their own ideas or alternatively can present B's. This helps to 'sharpen up' listening skills and can be used as a safe preliminary to group discussion.

Brainstorming
Select an idea or theme and ask for as many comments and views as possible without prioritising them. This emphasises corporate creativity and that everyone has a valued and valuable contribution to make. If appropriate, the group can later structure the comments and views into categories and use as a basis for decision-making.

Nominations for success
Individuals can nominate each other for verbal or tangible praise for any success or personal achievement they have noticed.

Handouts
Group participants are each given a handout with a particular focus for comment and discussion.

Drama strategies
Drama techniques can be effectively used to help participants explore issues using past experiences and present levels of understanding. Role-play reflects a true valuing of the individual; precisely because the 'dynamic' is the individual. Through drama, participants can express hidden feelings, practise empathy, and understanding of others, try out new behaviours, explore social problems and the dynamics of group interaction. Use of mime can help with understanding the importance of body language. Drama also encourages the imagination, which in turn enhances playground play.

Questions A 'trigger' question is put to the group, with time given for participants to explore their personal responses.

Discussion Discussion requires the putting forward of more than one point of view. Discussion is essentially a 'give and take' activity of a highly reciprocal nature. Discussion requires the participants to be prepared to examine and be responsive to the different opinions put forward.

Reflection A deliberate co-operative task which encourages the group to reflect on the meanings underlying the experience they've just shared. It is a group negotiation for meaning.

Calming rituals Children's days are full of 'rush and stress' and they need to learn how to become calm and more aware of an inner, more peaceful self. In the circle, teachers can teach breathing exercises and introduce relaxation strategies to help children learn how to become calm and relaxed.

IDEAS FOR CLASS CIRCLE-TIME

The following ideas are provided to help teachers who are unused to initiating whole class Circle-Time Sessions. I have therefore emphasised the Golden Rules that could be drawn out and discussed after each activity. Please note though, that these activities are only suggestions. Some classes will have moved beyond the stage of needing to draw up or discuss Golden Rules. Once a class and its teacher gain confidence, they could decide to drop the activities altogether as the children decide what issues they want raised. As trust and self-discipline develops, the children can take turns to run the Circle-Time Sessions for themselves.

Note: At the bottom of each session plan, there is a reference to how the activities meet the requirements of the **English** National Cirriculum.

ROUNDS AND THE 'TALKING OBJECT' OR 'CONCH'

CTS

Aim   To share feelings, evaluate experience, develop talking and listening skills, find out about bullying, give teacher and pupils important feedback.

What to do   In a circle, everyone including the teacher completes a sentence e.g. " I don't like it when......" whilst holding the 'talking object', (e.g. a conch shell). If a child is stuck for what to say s/he can say 'pass'. The first person to start the circle gives another opportunity for all 'passes' to take their turn at the end of the round.

Examples of rounds

1. I get fed up at lunchtimes when...

2. I am afraid of...

3. I feel really happy when...

4. I was embarrassed when...

5. I like it when...

6. The best part of my weekend was...

7. I did not like it when...

8. I don't want people to call me...

Question   Would anyone like to hold the 'talking object' and talk about a particular problem they would like some help with?

Golden Rule   Do listen carefully to each other.

Attainment target 1   Level 1a, 2a, 2b, 2d.

CAN I HELP?

Aim To encourage children to identify any problems they would like help with. To help the class consider itself responsible for sorting out their own problems.

Question Ask the class if anyone has a problem they would like some help with; children are incredibly honest. Remind them of the rule that they cannot mention anyone's name in a negative way. Typical answers include, "I need help because I keep fighting", "I need help because I have no one to play with", "I need help because I don't get on with my work", " I need help because somebody keeps calling me names."

What to do Children who would like to help that child put up their hands. The child then looks around and says the name of a certain child. He or she responds by asking – "Would it help if I...?" "Would it help if you...?" e.g. "John, would it help if I came and asked you to play with me?", "Emma, would it help if you stopped winding people up first?"

The child who is being addressed then has to give their considered response to the suggestion, e.g. "No, I don't think I can ignore them", or "Yes, it would be nice if I could play with you", or "I'm not sure if that would help me."

The child and the class group then decide on an Action Plan for the week which can then be reviewed in next week's Circle-Time. At this time that child can congratulate or thank any children who have helped him or her.

Golden Rule Do be kind and help each other.

Attainment target 1 Level 1a, 1b, 1c, 2a, 2b, 2d.

I think circle meetings are important because they stop people fighting.

121

Aim To mix children up in a circle so they sit next to someone different. To trigger discussion on the need to be gentle.

What to do In a circle, all the children sit on chairs facing inwards with one child in the middle. The seated children are alternately labelled orange or lemon. The child in the middle calls a command "oranges", "lemons" or "fruit basket". The seated children respond by changing seats if their category is called. "Fruit basket" means all change seats. During the changeover the child in the middle tries to gain a seat. The child who is left then takes over the middle.

Question How many of you know you are getting rough now?

What will happen if we continue to push each other out of the way?

Note: Some children needing attention pretend not to see the empty chair they could run to. If they end up there twice they have to choose someone else in their place.

Expand The child left in the middle can say "All those who like animals", or "All of those who have blue eyes can change places". Then pair people A or B and ask them to find out what things they have at home in common.

Golden Rule Do be gentle.

Attainment target 1 Level 1a, 1c, 2a, 2d, 3b, 3c, 3d.

Aim   To help children understand that things they say can hurt other people's feelings.

What to do   In a circle, teacher reads the story of 'John's Day'. Large cut-out stars are given to one child and small pebbles to another. On the floor the teacher places two large card circles one for stars and the other for stones. Each time something nice happens to John, the child holding the stars places one in the star circle. Each time something bad happens to John, the child holding the stones places one in the stone circle. The other children help by prompting. At the end of the story the stars and the stones are added up to see which circle contains the most. Teacher asks children how the 'stars' and 'stones' affect people. How do 'boost ups' and 'put downs' make you feel?

Round   I don't like it when people say...

I like it when people say...

Game   First play the 'Mix 'em up' game. This will change the children's seating arrangements so that they are not next to friends.

Pairs   Divide children into pairs of A's and B's. Each child must tell their partner one thing that "I like about you".

Expand   Teacher can prepare gift tags for each child saying "I like your gift of......" Alternatively the children can make them and give them to each other. For example "I like your gift of making jokes!"

Discussion   How do we feel when people say hurtful things about us?

Golden Rule   Do say positive things to each other.

Attainment target 1   Level 1a, 1b, 1c, 2a, 2d, 3b, 3c.

> I think circle time is very good because you can discus your problems and then they will not call you names and they will not kick you and they will stop it all. And some times I got called web because my real name is Webster and some times Claire my friends say's I live in a spider - web and I do not like it.

BOOST UPS AND PUT DOWNS

John's day

One Thursday morning John woke earlier than usual. He wanted to be in the school football team, so he decided to get up and do some exercises to make himself fitter.

His sister Joanne, hearing the noise of John exercising came into his room. "What are you doing? she asked him.

"I'm trying to get fit, so that I'm chosen for the football team?"

"I shouldn't bother", Joanne replied "They won't choose a slow, dozey twit like you."

At breakfast, Joanne said to their mother, "John's been exercising, he actually thinks he might get picked for the football team. Fat chance I say."

"You keep exercising", John's mother told him, "If you don't try you never succeed. I'm sure, if you put your mind to it, you'll have as much chance as anybody else."

At school, John told his best friend Alex what had happened. "Don't take any notice of Joanne," said Alex "older sisters are like that. I think you might get into the team, you're very good in defence."

The first lesson was maths. John couldn't find his book anywhere. "I see John Thorpe is last to be ready again", said his teacher. "Really John, I wish you would be a bit more organised".

At last John found his book, right at the bottom of his desk, under a pile of loose papers, but when he opened it at the right page, he couldn't remember how to do the sums.

He went up to his teacher's desk "Please Miss Davies", he said "I've forgotten how to do these".

"You'd forget your head if it wasn't attached to your body" said Miss Davies and all the other children laughed. Well as you've wasted so much time this morning you can stay in for 5 minutes at break to make it up."

"What a dumbo!" hissed Sally Peters to John as he made his way back to his desk.

The lesson after break was English. The class watched a video and then Miss Davies asked them some questions about it. John put up his hand several times and at last Miss Davies chose him.

"I bet he gets it wrong", Sally Peters said to her neighbour, so that John could hear. But he didn't. John gave the correct answer and Miss Davies said to him "Well done John for being so observant!"

John was very keen to get into the playground after lunch so that he could join in the game of football. He was delayed a bit because he was helping to clear away the lunch things and when he did get outside the game was in full swing.

"You're too late to join in", said David "we've already got two teams".

"Anyway", said Peter Hall "I don't want him on my team he's useless!"

Mrs Harper the lunchtime supervisor noticed John was looking miserable and asked him what the matter was. "Oh what a shame", she said when John told her, "I'm sure we could sort something out." She called the football boys over to her. "You know boys, it's very sad when you're left out of something you really enjoy. Would one of you let John have a go?"

"He can have my place for a while", volunteered Simon Phelps.

Peter Hall was not so kind though, "You're a sneaky, tell-tale-tit" he said to John, "I'm just glad you're not on my team."

The class were painting pictures of a jungle in the afternoon. John had used lots of bright colours and was pleased with his effort. Sally Peters came over to look at what he had done, "Ugh!" she said, that looks a real mess, my 3 year old brother could do better." John felt very upset and did not like his picture after that.

At the end of the day, John was eager to get home. It had been a horrible day and he felt quite miserable. In his haste to be gone he accidentally knocked over one of the younger children. "You clumsy oaf", shouted the headteacher, who had been watching "can't you look where you're going?" John felt very near to tears, he just couldn't do anything right and it seemed as if everybody had something unkind to say to him.

"WELL DONE" OR "GOOD TRY"

Aim To develop imagination, memory and self-control skills, to help children praise each other.

What to do In a circle, one child is given an object e.g. a ruler and has to mime an action using the ruler as another object e.g. an umbrella, a comb. The other children put up their hands to guess what the object is being used as. The child doing the mime chooses a child then says "Well done," if they get it right or "Good try," if they get it wrong.

Expand A selection of objects is placed in the centre of the circle. Children choose one object and mime using this object as something different.

Choose an article, such as a chair, and encourage the children to use the object in diverse actions regardless of size e.g. use chair as vacuum clearer, shopping bag, hair brush.

Discussion How often do I say well done or good try? Is there anyone in this class who you have noticed has improved their work or behaviour recently?

Expand Children are asked to put up their hands and nominate someone in their class whose behaviour has recently improved either at classtime or lunchtimes, (but they can't nominate a best friend), and look over to them and say, "I'd like to say well done to you, Robert, because you have stopped fighting in the playground..."All the class smile at, and clap the nominated person.

Golden Rule Always say positive things to each other.

Attainment target 1 Level 1 a, 1b, 1c, 2a, 2d, 3b, 3c, 4c.

Aim To help children appreciate and accept the differences between people.

What to do In a circle all children have a clear piece of white card with their name at the top. Two children (each go around half the circle) take an ink or paint pad around to the other children who each press their thumb onto the pad and make a thumb print on the piece of white card.

In small groups The children examine the thumb print to see how each one is different. Then reform into large circle where the teacher goes around the circle putting them into pairs, (A or B).

Pairs A and B decide on two things they both like very much – now send a conch around with each person from the pair saying the things they decide they like. All others – as individuals – can say "yes" loudly if they too like the same thing – but they're not allowed to say "no", "yuck" – or give negative body language if they don't .

Golden Rule Do accept people's differences.

Expand Each child in turn holds up his/her thumb and tells an imaginary story about it eg. "I used this thumb to pull a plum out of a pie." "This thumb pushed a button and sent a rocket to the moon."

Attainment target 1 Level 1a, 1b, 1c, 2a, 2b, 2d, 2e, 3a, 3b, 3c, 4c.

> I think circle time is for thanking people. Saying sorry to people and helping to slove their problems

GIVE A GOOD WISH

Aim   To encourage children to think about the needs and wishes of others.

What to do   In pairs (but not close friends together) children write or draw a wish for their partners, thinking of something they might really like. It need not be an object, e.g. "I wish you could be an astronaut and fly to the moon." The wishes are then exchanged, read and discussed.

Expand   All children hang up a stocking with their names on. On separate pieces of paper, each child must write down a positive statement about the five children sitting to their right and put the statements into the correct stockings. Everyone can then read what has been written about them.

Discussion   What sort of things, other than objects, make people happy? What nice "ideals" could we wish for? (kindness, gentleness, consideration etc.)

Golden Rule   Be kind.

Attainment target 1   Level 1a, 1c, 2a, 2b, 3a, 3c, 4c.

FINDER OF THE TREASURE

CTS

Aim	To help children think about what they want to achieve and what stops them. To aid concentration and listening skills.
What to do	The children make up a story about treasure:- what it is, who it belongs to (eg. a pirate and his treasure, a magician and his spell book, a monster and his gold).
	In a circle the children place a variety of obstacles, (upturned chairs, pieces of scrunched up newspaper etc.) A chair is placed in the centre for the keeper of the treasure to sit on and the treasure (something noisy such as keys or bells) is placed under the chair. The keeper is blindfolded and a chosen 'finder' tries to negotiate the obstacles, capture the treasure and return with it to their seat. If the keeper hears the finder s/he shouts "Stop" and points in the direction of the noise. If correct another 'finder' attempts to capture the treasure. If a finder is successful s/he can become the keeper or elect another child to be keeper.
Expand	When a finder is detached s/he can lie on the floor and become another obstacle.
Discussion	What kind of treasure or goal do we look for in life?
	What obstacles prevent us from reaching our goals?
	How can we overcome these obstacles?
Golden Rule	Do concentrate on your task.
Attainment target 1	Level 1a, 1b, 1c, 2a, 2b, 3a, 4c.

GETTING TO KNOW YOU

Aim	To improve listening and talking skills, self-awareness and self-disclosure.
What to do	In small groups, children get into pairs,(A and B)with the person sitting next to them, A becomes the interviewer and questions B to find out as much about him/her as possible. A then reports back to the group as much as can be recalled about B. The process is then reversed.
Expand	Children can draw up a list of questions beforehand. Each child makes a Booster Poster about their partner,(see p132)
Discussion	What interesting new things did you discover about your partner?
Golden Rule	Do listen carefully to each other.
Attainment target 1	Level 1a, 2a, 3c, 4c.

> I think circle meetings are important because you can tork too eachother

COPY THE LEADER

Aim	To develop concentration, eye-contact and have fun.
What to do	In a circle, a leader begins a movement which is copied by all the circle. The leader then provides a new movement which is again copied.
Expand	One player a 'detective' stands outside the circle and a new leader is chosen. When the action is in progress, the detective must come into the middle of the circle and try and identify the leader.
Discussion	What helps us to be accurate in copying the movement? When and why is concentration important in school?
Golden Rule	Do concentrate on your task.
Attainment target 1	Level 1a, 1c, 2a, 2c, 3b, 3c, 4c.

WHO HAS GONE?

Aim To develop group awareness, questioning techniques and observation.

What to do In a circle, children sit with eyes closed or blindfolded and not touching each other. A chosen child touches another who quietly leaves the circle. The remainder, still with eyes blindfolded, are allowed to ask the first child a set number of questions(excluding names) before attempting to guess the identity of the missing child. If the guess is incorrect, a further question session follows.

Expand In pairs, children study the appearance of their partners, then turn back to back and slightly alter their appearance eg. push up sleeve, roll down a sock, unbutton cardigan. They then face each other again and try to guess what change had been made. Alternatively, one child chooses the identity of a famous person and the remainder are allowed twenty questions eliciting only "yes" or "no" answers to guess who it is.

Discussion What helped us think of good questions? Discuss observation and the idea of specific and useful questions.

Golden Rule Do notice everyone is special.

Attainment target 1 Level 1a, 1c, 2a, 2d, 3c, 4c.

ZOOM AND EEK

Aim	To develop awareness of the importance of sharing together.
What to do	One child starts the car going around the circle by saying "Zoom" and turning their head quickly to the person next to them on the right. The next person repeats this action and it continues around the circle until a child says "Eek". The car then changes direction and the "Zoom" sound goes the other way until the next "Eek". At first the teacher can say "Zoom" and "Eek" and then the children can determine the car's movements themselves. Some children can be selfish in their use of the "Eek" and can confine the action to only one part of the circle. This then needs to be highlighted.
Discussion	How can we be considerate and ensure that all children share in the action and enjoyment? How can we be more considerate of other people's feelings in general?
Golden Rule	Do be considerate of other people's feelings.
Attainment target 1	Level 1a, 1c, 2d, 3c, 4c.

IF I WERE

Aim	To develop self-awareness, enhance speaking skills and help express feelings in a safe situation.
What to do	In a circle each participant finishes a statement such as "If I were a bird I would want to be a .... because ....
Expand	Use other categories e.g. famous people, animals, colours. This activity can be done in small groups or pairs within the circle. Ideas can be written down and used in drama or art.
Discussion	What more would I like to say about myself, my dreams, ambitions and hopes?
Attainment target 1	Level 1a, 1c, 2c, 2b, 3c, 4c.

SHARE YOUR PROBLEMS

CTS

Aim   To develop communication and trust. To help children realise that a range of behaviour options are open to them. To help them realise the answer to problems often lies with them.

What to do   If a problem arises at any time in the group a circle is formed and ways to help overcome the problem are brainstormed. A strategy is decided on by individuals or the group and a Circle-Time Session is planned for when it can be evaluated.

Expand   Children can ask for help with a work or behaviour problem, (as long as they don't give names) of other children they are cross with, using phrases like "somebody hurt me" or " people gang up on me".

Example   Children may say "I need help to stop fighting."

Golden Rule   Help each other.

Attainment target 1   Level 1a, 1c, 2a, 2d, 3c, 3d, 4c.

---

circle meeting

I think circle time is good because you can learn from it and you can tell other People your problems.

I CAN HEAR YOU

Aim   To develop listening skills and help achieve silence. To develop gentleness towards each other.

What to do   In a circle, two children are chosen and blindfolded to play the hunter and the prey. The hunter tries to capture the prey whilst the other children guide them back into the centre of the circle using contact with the palms of their hands. The game takes place in silence

Discussion   What helped the hunter find their prey? Why is listening important and useful?

Golden Rule   Do listen carefully to each other.
Do be gentle.

Attainment target 1   Level 1a, 1b, 2a, 3c, 4c.

I think circle meetings are a good idea because you can talk about your problems. I think younger children and older children should have them aswell.

BOOSTER POSTER

Aim   To boost self-esteem and encourage knowledge of others.

What to do   Take a photograph of each child and attach them to a large piece of card. Each child writes all the things about him/herself that they want other people to know and these are placed under the relevant photos.

Expand   Each child can design a personal coat of arms and include in the design illustrations of activities they feel they are good at.
Acrostic – each child's name is written vertically and a sentence or phrase describing a positive attribute is written beside each letter.

e.g. Jane :   **J**oins in well

          Actively helps people

          Never says unkind things

          Excellent at helping.

Each child can make a silhouette of themselves to which other children can stick a positive comments about them.

Discussion   Everyone is unique and different, everybody is good at something.

Golden Rule   Do accept people's differences.

Attainment target 1   Level 1a, 1c, 2a, 2d, 3c, 4c.

SILENCE IS GOLDEN

CTS

Aim — To develop concentration, achieve silence and share goals.

What to do — In a circle, a musical instrument is passed from one person to the next, trying not to make a sound.

Expand — Children shut their eyes whilst the teacher uses various objects to make different sounds which the children have to identify.

Discussion: — What helped us achieve silence? Co-operation and sharing are important for everyone.

When do we need/like silence?

Golden Rule — We all need to share silent times.

Attainment target 1 — Level 1a, 2d, 3c, 4c.

I think circle meetings are important because it makes us a quiet

CLIC
CLAC
CLIC

SEND A RIPPLE

Aim To help concentration.

What to do In a circle, the teacher explains that s/he is the rain by waving their fingers. Participants must pass the action on around the circle. The teacher is then thunder and mimes this by slapping his or her knees. Again the action is passed around the circle. The teacher then alternates rain and thunder movements until the next movements reaches their place in the circle. Finally the teacher 'brings out the sun' by folding his or her arms and this action is also passed around the circle.

Discussion What helped us know the correct movement to make? Why is concentration important in your school work?

Golden Rule Do concentrate on your given task.

Attainment target 1 Level 1a, 1b, 2d, 3c, 4c.

SMILE OR FROWN

Aim To help children make their feelings explicit and become more reflective. To provide useful information and different perspectives for the teacher.

What to do In a circle each child says what they did or did not enjoy about the day, or teaching session. Sentences to complete can include:

"I enjoyed ...."

"I did not like ...."

"It was nice when. ......"

Try to end with positive statements.

Discussion How could the children and teacher improve teaching sessions?

Golden Rule Do listen carefully to each other.

Attainment target 1 1a, 1c, 2d, 3c, 4c.

STORY ROUNDABOUT

Aim To enhance listening skills, concentration, language development and memory.

What to do In a circle, the children make up a class story. Each child adds a word or one sentence in turn.

Expand Children can volunteer to re-tell an old favourite with their own adaptations and alterations. The rest of the class can join in with "oohs", "aahs", "hisses", "hoorays" etc.

Golden Rule Do listen very carefully.

Attainment target 1 Level 1a, 1b, 1c, 2a, 2b, 2d, 3a, 3b, 3c, 4c.

SHARE A CHAIR

Aim To encurge co-operation and sharing.

What to do The children are alternately labelled A and B, on the commands of "A" or "B" the children with the appropriate letter change seats, so that the seating arrangements becomes altered. Each child then pairs up with the child on their right. Every pair has a chair and must find as many different ways as possible of both occupying the chair with their feet off the ground.

Discussion What do we need to help us think of different positions? Typical answers include sharing, being helpful and careful with one other.

Golden Rule Do be gentle.

Attainment target 1 Level 1a, 1c, 2a, 2d, 3c, 4c.

Aim	To stimulate imagination, to improve speaking and listenings skills and to enhance self-esteem.
What to do	The teacher sets the scene by telling children they are expert botanists attending a conference because they have each discovered a new plant. Each child describes their plant and talks about it. Each person gets a clap for their discovery.
Expand	An alternative storyline could be: a convention for magicians who have each invented a new spell, or explorers who had discovered something on an island.
Discussion	What did you enjoy most about this game?
	We are all good at something eg. reading, a sport, looking after a pet, helping at home.
Round	"One thing I'm good at is ...."
Golden Rule	Do listen to everyone.
Attainment target 1	Level 1a, 1b, 1c, 2a, 2b, 2c, 2d, 3a, 3b, 3c, 4b, 4c.

I think circle meetings are nice because you helppepot.

SIMON SAYS

Aim To enhance communications skills, concentration and to trigger discussion on what it feels like when we make a mistake.

What to do In a circle, a leader, 'Simon' is chosen to give commands whilst demonstrating actions, e.g. hands on heads. If the prefix "Simon says" is put before a command, all the children copy the action. If the order is given without the prefix, the group must not imitate the action. The 'No put-downs' rule must apply, so children don't laugh at others' mistakes.

Expand Change leaders. Leaders can hand over leadership by saying "Simon says follow ....." The leader can offer only verbal instructions without the mime.

Discussion What helped us to follow the leader correctly?

Golden Rule Do allow people to make mistakes.

Attainment target 1 Level 1a, 1b, 2a, 3b, 3c, 4c.

> I think Circle time is good because is's fun and good and you can say any of your worry's and you can help others and you play game's.

(CTS) CAN I TRY AND UNDERSTAND?

Aim To develop empathy and sensitivity towards others. To help children express their feelings anonymously in a non-threatening way through role-play.

What to do In a circle, the teacher identifies a particular feeling, eg worry. The children complete a written sentence "I am worried that ...." The sentences are all put into a container and each child takes a turn to withdraw a sentence at random and read it out, with feeling, as if the reader had written that sentence themselves.

Expand Once the child has read the sentence, s/he tries to talk about the worry (fear, happiness etc) in more detail using all their imagination, as if the worry was their own.

Discussion What sort if things make us feel worried? How can we help each other not to feel worried?

Golden Rule Do consider other people's feelings.

Attainment target 1 Level 1a, 1b, 2a, 2d, 3b, 3c, 4c.

(CTS) CALMING TIMES

Aim To encourage imagination, relaxation and a stress-free time as a group.

What to do The children lie in the circle, heads towards the middle, feet to the outside, in a relaxed position with their eyes closed. Use one of the fantasy journeys to encourage the children to enjoy an imaginative experience.

Pairs Afterwards, in pairs, take turns to tell each other about their journeys.

Expand Children can write stories or poems that can be shared in the next Circle-Time Session.

CALMING TIMES

Fantasy journey 1

Imagine that you are in a canoe going down a river. What does it feel like? – rocking, swaying, bobbing up and down? What sounds can you hear? – sound of water, birds, (You can use a sound effects tape of water.) What can you see as the canoe moves along? Trees, flowers, birds, animals? The canoe passes a beautiful jungle. What can you see in the jungle? (The journey can be expanded to include all sorts of sights, sounds or feelings.)

> Gradually bring the children 'back' from the fantasy by gently reminding them who they are and that they are using their imagination, that they are now back in their classroom. Tell them to stretch and relax and slowly sit back on their chairs.

Fantasy journey 2

Imagine you are a bird sitting in a nest. Think about the nest, what does it look like, imagine the tree that the nest is in, what shaped leaves does it have? You are going on a journey, think about standing up in your nest and flexing your wings – feel the power in your wings to lift you out of the nest. You are soaring and swooping in the sky round and around you fly. What can you see below you? Now you are gently gliding along on the warm air currents, you feel free and happy, very relaxed. The sun is warm and kind on your back, it makes you feel good. Everything looks bright and lovely, think of all the bright colours and nice shapes you can see and feel the warm air swooshing past you as you fly. Where do you want to go? Think of what you are going to do and see as you fly around.

> Gradually bring the children 'back' from the fantasy by gently reminding them who they are and that they are using their imagination, that they are now back in their classroom. Tell them to stretch and relax and slowly sit back on their chairs.

OPENING AND CLOSING ACTIVITIES

It is useful to have a selection of activities that 'open' and 'close' Circle-Time Sessions. These are primarily to draw the group together through having fun.

Wink murder

In a circle a detective is chosen and leaves the room for a minute while a murderer is chosen. The detective returns to the room and stands in the centre of the circle. The murderer must chose a victim and wink at them whereupon the victim 'dies'. The murderer must try to avoid detection (winking when the detective's back is turned) and the detective must watch the other children's actions and try and guess who the murderer is.

Tangles

The children close their eyes and move towards one another. Every child finds one hand to hold in each of their hands. The children then open their eyes and must try and untangle themselves to form one large circle without letting go of each other.

My class

Each child says a positive word about what being in the class makes them feel e.g. happy, fun, strong.

Goodbye song

The children sing a song that they all know to end the Circle-time Session.

Squeeze of kindness

Children pass a hand squeeze of kindness around the circle.

Sound waves

In a circle, one person makes a sound, which is then copied by each child around the circle in turn. Sounds can be made quite complicated once children are used to the game, or each child can slightly change the noise.

Something good

Each child tells something good or pleasant that has happened to them during the last week.

Pass the frisbee

Children stand in a circle. One child places a frisbee or similar object between their knees. The frisbee must be passed from child to child, between the knees, around the circle, without using hands. A child can only use hands to pick up the frisbee if it is dropped.

Section 5

Circle-Time Sessions and parental involvement

INVOLVING PARENTS

If a school decides to pursue a whole school policy on self-esteem and positive behaviour, it has more chance of being successful if it takes on this task in real partnership with parents.

Parents play a crucial role in enhancing their children's self-esteem, in setting behaviour boundaries and in reinforcing the academic and social initiatives being promoted within the school. Much of the good self-esteem building work done by parents at home can be 'undone' by teachers and, similarly, much of the self-esteem input from the school can be undermined at home.

Parenthood is a difficult and vulnerable task. Statistics show that it is becoming even more complex, due to the pressures of modern day living. Many parents are having to perform numerous roles and cope with so many demands on their time that often they suffer from low self-esteem, which can in turn, lead to them to respond negatively towards their children. All the workshops I have held with parents have highlighted just how many individuals are struggling against great odds. Through Circle-Time I have explored with them, how best they can help motivate their children and enhance their self-esteem within the constraints and pressures of everyday life. But it is important that teachers know and respect the difficulties faced by parents and learn to look for the positive strengths and qualities they offer in order to create a fruitful partnership.

Some schools find that it is a good idea to initially acquaint parents with the values of the school through the formulation of a Home-School Contract. This document, for them to sign, can form the basis for future discussions.

EXAMPLES OF A HOME-SCHOOL CONTRACT

Name of School

THE HOME-SCHOOL PARTNERSHIP

All the children need a positive and supportive relationship between home and school to enhance their attitude, behaviour and motivation. In order to achieve this parents need to be informed and involved in discussion about curriculum and assessment.

Your child only has one school career, and for this to be the best that can achieved, the Home-School partnership must be seen as a real and lively relationship promoting the highest expectations between school, parents and pupils.

Pupil and Parent expectations of the school	School expectations of parents and pupils
A safe, well-ordered, caring environment in which learning can take place.	A safe, caring home environment which allows pupils to develop positive attitudes towards school.
The pupil valued as an individual.	To support the self-esteem and behaviour policy.
Challenging programmes of teaching. Guidance and opportunities for pupils to achieve their full potential.	A supportive attitude which complements the work of the school and will allow the child to benefit from education.
Early warnings of problems concerning work, behaviour or relationships.	Early contact with the school to discuss matters relating to pupils' progress, behaviour or happiness.
Regular information about academic and social progress and performance.	Participation in agreed procedures about progress and attainment.
Regular opportunities to express views on wider issues which can be recognised and valued.	Acceptance of the school ethos and positive support of the teachers' role.

We, the parents and the school, have a shared commitment to:

Help our young people become happy, capable and confident, able to take responsibility for their own futures and to respect and care for other people.

Give the life of the school a priority of shared interest and enthusiasm.

Provide mutual support for young people as they face the problems of growing up in today's society.

Signed Headteacher..

Signed Parent/Guardian...

Pupils' rights

In so far as possible the school will seek to:-

1. Promote the child's right to be safe and learn in a comfortable and friendly environment.

2. Be listened to and respected.

3. Be given opportunities to achieve potential commensurate with his/her abilities.

4. Receive encouragement and experience success.

Parents' rights

In so far as possible the school will seek to promote the parents' rights to:-

1. Be partners in their children's education.

2. Receive written information about school policies relevant to parents.

3. Be consulted about and given ongoing information about the educational progress of their child.

Teachers' rights

In so far as possible the school will seek to promote the teacher's right to:

1. Be safe and teach in a comfortable and friendly environment.

2. Be listened to and respected.

3. A programme of personal and professional staff development.

4. Adequate resources.

5. Pastoral and professional support within the school and from appropriate outside agencies.

Signed Pupil...

Signed Parent...

Signed School...

RAISING THE SELF-ESTEEM OF PARENTS

It is in the school's interest to help parents feel that they are valued and have an important role to play in their children's schooling. It is important that schools recognise that some parents received negative experiences at school and are quite fearful of getting involved again.

There are many ways that parents can be encouraged to be more involved in school life:-

○ Involve parents in activities that can utilise their skills. Send out a a list of skills you need help with and ask them to tick any they could offer.

○ Use a parent/teacher reading scheme to encourage parents to get involved in the reading process.

○ Praise the parent through the child by taking time to tell parents the good things that you've noticed.

○ Involve parents in reviews of your self-esteem and behaviour policy and in any other decisions that need to be taken.

○ Send positive notes home.

○ Organise enjoyable social events to which parents are invited. (Family games or quiz evenings have proven very popular!)

○ Invite parents into school to watch Circle-Time.

○ Nip outside at the end of the day for a warm word.

○ Be prepared to do occasional home visits.

○ Listen to their concerns and feelings.

Parents have the right to 'Good News" about their children

Every parent has the right to hear regular 'good news' about their children. Yet, more often than not, they are only contacted when a problem arises. Hence many parental visits to school are defensive and anxious occasions. Such parents would feel less defensive when a school notices 'bad' things about their children if they could trust the school to also regularly recognise and value the good things in them.

For this reason, it is vital that a school's Incentives Policy should include tangible rewards which can be taken or sent home for the parents to see. In this way, parents will have proof that the school is fair in recognising both the good and bad in their children.

Such rewards could include:-

○ smiley stickers

○ seals of approval

○ labels

○ certificates

○ congratulationary stationery

○ P.A.C.T. (Parents in Association with Children and Teachers) – any scheme involving daily written comments from parent, child and teacher.

Keeping parents informed

Parents should be informed from the outset of a school's plans for policy making, but during a school's initial stages of developing a policy, the staff will need to concentrate their own efforts on the issues involved. However, once they are confident that they fully understand the need for a whole school policy and are able to implement it as a team, parents can be invited in to Circle-Time Sessions.

Below is an example of how one school informed parents about its policy for promoting positive behaviour and self-esteem.

NEWTOWN COUNTY JUNIOR SCHOOL

Dear Parents,

School Policy for Promoting Behaviour and Self-Esteem

The staff have spent the past eighteen months preparing a policy for developing the children's self-esteem and a positive attitude towards behaviour, believing that children respond best to a supportive and caring approach.

It is a policy based firmly in using rewards and praise and developing the children's self-esteem by highlighting good behaviour. However, the policy also recognises that there is a need for sanctions and these are clearly laid down. We hope very soon to be able to share the whole policy with you once it has been printed.

This letter is to tell you about two sets of rewards we are using at present, so you have a clear picture of what is happening in school.

Reward Stickers – These are given out by staff and dinner ladies to reward all sorts of good behaviour – politeness, helpfulness, kindness, good effort, hard work, etc. If your child wears one home at the end of the day please give praise and ask what it was given for – s/he will have done something good.

We feel this is a really good and positive link between school and home and know you will support us with it.

"Hive of Achievements" – Your child may already have received a "hexagon". These are awarded for a special achievement, for example for consistently good work or effort or for being particularly kind or helpful. They are displayed in the hall at Newtown and a copy kept on the child's record until s/he leaves us at the end of year 6.

We hope every child will receive at least two or three hexagons during each year, please understand that they are not given freely and really need to be earned.

I am sure you will agree that these are positive developments to which we know the children are responding very well. We look forward to sharing the whole school policy with you in time.

With best wishes.

Yours sincerely

Richard Craft. Headteacher.

INVOLVING PARENTS THROUGH CIRCLE-TIME

One of the best ways of involving parents in a school's self-esteem and behaviour policy is to invite them in to school for a Circle-Time Session on the issues involved. A letter can be sent out to all parents specifying a date for such a meeting.

Help your child do well at school

Dear Parent,

Your child only has one school career and our aim in this school is to help each child to be happy, confident and able to develop to his/her full potential.

We know that you share this aim with us and urge you to attend a meeting at the School on .... to discuss how you as parents, and we, as teachers, can work together to promote your child's happiness and help him/her reach his/her full learning potential.

Yours sincerely

A very effective way of further persuading parents to come to this meeting, is to allow the children themselves to write a subsequent invitation to take home the day before the meeting. This will act as a reminder and because it is more personal, exerts a subtle pressure on the parents to attend! Prepare the hall in as welcoming a way as possible bearing in mind that when the parents see that large circle of chairs their anxiety will be increased!

Aim   To involve parents in the aims of the school to promote self-esteem and positive behaviour.

Discussion   If I asked each of you to speak about any chosen topic in this circle, how would you feel?

Typical answers are:
very nervous, butterflies in stomach, terrified.

What makes you feel nervous in this circle? What are you afraid of?

Typical answers are:
saying the wrong thing, getting tongue-tied, looking foolish, too many people looking at me.

Where do these feelings come from, when have you 'learnt' to be anxious?

Typical answers are:
being put-down-at school, being laughed at, adults making sarcastic or belittling remarks about us when we were young.

Round   What do we want for our children?

Typical answers are:
Happiness, confidence, self-fulfilment.

Facilitator   The answers you have given are the same aims as we the school staff want for your children. To achieve these goals we have begun work on our self-esteem policy which we would like to share with you.

At this point the school could briefly outline the initiatives that they are going to include in their incentives, sanctions and lunchtime policy.

ENHANCING SELF-ESTEEM IN YOUR CHILDREN

CTS

Aim	To raise parents' awareness of the importance of self-esteem.
Discussion	How can you as parents, support us at home by boosting your children's self-esteem? What can you as parents, do to enhance your child's self-esteem at home and how can you work with teachers towards a common aim?
In small circles	Each participant contributes ways in which they help boost the self-esteem of their children at home. One of the groups notes these down in a list.
In a large circle	A spokesman from each group takes it in turns around the circle to read one item from his/her list. (If this item is included on any other person's list it is crossed off) so that all the ideas are pooled.
Handout 1	**Some parents ideas.**
Action Plan	Facilitator asks parents 'what can the school do to help you'?
Handout 2	Parents take home the two letters, one from children to parents and one from parents to children and form an action plan to help their children.
Handout 3	They can also take the handout 3, **What is self-esteem?** to read and reflect on.
Development	The facilitator collects the lists made in the small circles and includes them, and parents' comments about this circle workshop for the next parents' newsletter. This will encourage more parents to attend a subsequent meeting. A further Circle-Time Session should be held for parents to acquaint them with any further incentives and sanctions policies drawn up by the school. explaining fully how the various measures are implemented and why. This meeting will also acquaint parents with how their views are support have been included in the school's self-esteem and behaviour policy and document the ways in which they can become actively involved in school life.

Some parents' ideas:-

- ○ Give lots of praise for the good things your child achieves.

- ○ Give lots of hugs and cuddles and tell your children how much you love them.

- ○ Expect and allow your child to make mistakes – this is part of growing up – don't make a 'big thing' about it.

- ○ Accept that your child has a right to his/her own opinions even if they are different from your own.

- ○ Teach your child responsibility by allowing him/her to do useful jobs.

- ○ Allow your child freedom of choice in selected areas – ie. clothes, spending pocket money.

- ○ Ensure that punishments are fair and relevant.

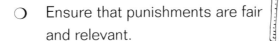

- ○ Be consistent – set secure boundaries for acceptable behaviour and make sure that your child knows the consequences of overstepping these boundaries.

- ○ Don't be prejudiced about your child's behaviour – allow room for him/her to change, learn to show trust.

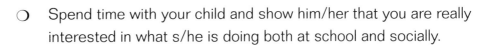

- ○ Spend time with your child and show him/her that you are really interested in what s/he is doing both at school and socially.

- ○ Don't dismiss your child's worries as trivial or stupid, they are very real to him/her.

- ○ Try to understand your child's world at their level. It is very easy to forget as an adult what is important, relevant or worrying for a child.

Letter 1

Dear Mum and Dad

You're always telling me how you want me to behave and what you want me to do, well now I'm going to turn the tables and tell you what is really important to me and what I would like from you.

1. I want to be loved and accepted for their person I am, I hate it when you tell me how good other children are, it makes me feel rejected and useless.

2. When I make mistakes or do something wrong remember I'm only human – don't go over the top, forgive me quickly – I need your love.

3. If you do something wrong, try and say sorry – you expect this from me.

4. Don't nag me, because I just 'switch off' when you do.

5. Keep your word, when you break your promises I feel 'let down'.

6. Don't keep changing the rules because I just don't know where I stand if you do.

7. Please don't tell me off in front of others, it makes me feel really small and I resent you for it.

8. I don't really mean it when I say I hate you, It's just the anger talking.

9. Ouch! This one hurts, but don't give me my own way all the time. I don't really expect to have everything I want, but I like to 'push' and see how for I can go. Every time you say "alright, one more chance" I know you are weakening.

10. Sometimes I whine or have 'headaches' for attention. I just want you to take notice of me and give me some time.

11. Try and understand my fears and anxieties. They might seem trivial to you, but they are very real to me and I need you to recognise their importance and help me deal with them.

12. I'm not as daft as you seem to think and I know when you're having a bad time, so please don't hide things from me when they are going wrong. Let me know simply what is happening.

13. Lastly, I love hugs and cuddles and sharing special things given to me – please spare the time for me.

Letter 2

Dear Children,

Well, you've certainly put us straight about a few things, in your letter. It's such a long time since I was your age and I had forgotten what is was like and how I felt. But I intend to do my best to be more aware and understanding in future.

I will:-

1. Try to practice what I preach and show you, by good example, how you should treat others.

2. Expect and allow you to make mistakes, encourage you to learn from them and forgive you quickly if you hurt our feelings.

3. Listen to and respect your personal views and remember that you are an individual in your own right.

4. Try not to compare you unfavourably with other children, knowing how 'threatened' we feel if you tell us how 'good' other parents are.

5. Help you towards self-reliance by trusting your judgement and giving you more responsibility when you can handle it.

6. Try and understand 'your world', what is important to you and what worries you and not dismiss anything as trivial.

7. Try and remember to praise all the good things you do and kindnesses you show.

8. Try to remember to show our love through cuddles and affection.

9. Try and encourage your feelings of self-worth by showing that we love, value and accept the unique person you are.

What is self-esteem?

○ Self-esteem is the inner picture we all have of ourselves. It is the value we give to our strengths and our weaknesses.

○ We have low self-esteem if we think we are useless, incompetent, unpopular and of little use to society.

○ If we have sound self-esteem we know we are capable, competent, liked and valued, we believe we can lead useful lives in society.

○ Self-esteem is shaped from an early age by the important adults in a child's life. Too much criticism, too many don'ts, too few cuddles, too little praise and encouragement when we are young leads to low self-esteem and feelings of failure.

○ A child who feels a failure may have trouble making friends, fitting in, doing the best they can.

○ A child who has sound self-esteem has a better chance of being successful in all areas of school life and of being confident to learn new things.

○ It is helpful for all children if the important adults in their life work together to share the same values and expectations.

○ Parents and teachers working together towards the same goals, can do much to build a child's self-esteem and make their school life happier and more fulfilled.

Appendix 1

**St Dunstan C.E. Junior School
self-esteem and positive behaviour policy**

(Developed by all adults and children
in the school community)

ST DUNSTAN C.E. JUNIOR SCHOOL SELF-ESTEEM AND POSITIVE BEHAVIOUR POLICY
(Developed by all adults and children in the school community)

Introduction

Low self-esteem affects behaviour, learning and relationships.

Self-esteem is the personal picture that we have of ourselves – our strengths and our limitations. This self-image is built by all the positive or negative responses of the people with whom we come into contact. Every child needs praise, success, recognition and affection.

A child can accept learning challenges and failure if s/he can draw upon the above resources.

A child with low self-esteem either resorts to negative attention seeking behaviour or withdraws, which in turn negatively affects his/her learning and/or relationships and becomes a negative, self-fulfilling cycle. Our job as teachers is to make sure no child/teacher is trapped in a negative relationship.

OUR POSITIVE BEHAVIOUR AND SELF-ESTEEM FLOW CHART AS DEVELOPED BY JENNY MOSLEY

CIRCLE-TIME

⇩

GOLDEN RULES

⇩

INCENTIVES

⇩

SANCTIONS

⇩

DINNER TIME POLICY

⇩

CHILDREN 'BEYOND' – INTO CONTRACTING

⇩

CONTRACT WITH TEACHERS/PARENTS

⇩

ASSESSMENT

⇩

CONTAINMENT

⇩

STAFF SUPPORT

Circle-Time

The children and staff will be seated comfortably, in a circle, so that everyone can be seen by everyone else.

When the talking object, ie shell, stone, etc is passed around only the person holding it may speak. If you do not wish to speak, you must say "Pass". Items for discussion might be:

All the things which make me happy
Playground experiences which make me sad

Issues which arise may then be explored in more depth. The talking object creates an open forum and children who are reluctant to talk in a classroom discussion will participate. Some children have no expectation of taking such a role. Equally it helps other children to control their genuine desire to talk/interrupt/control the discussion.

Circle-Time is a pleasant, comfortable time, when the class comes together for thought, enjoyment and self-congratulations. Problems can be discussed openly, either a whole class problem, or an individual one, and solved with the participation of the whole group. The emphasis in on help and not blame.

The group can congratulate itself on achievements either as a whole or individuals. Praise and rewards can be handed out by any members of the group.

Skills of listening, looking and thinking are highlighted in circle games.

Topics for discussion and comment can cover anything, ie school work, classroom behaviour and rules, dinnertime, playtime, travelling to and from school, interests at home and news, world events, worries, etc. Discussion is controlled which makes it difficult for children to just complain/tell tales. The onus is put on the individual to solve problems rather than just voice them. Children learn to recognise anti-social behaviour and its effect on others.

Circle work must have structure eg, 1 round, 1 game 1 open discussion, 1 fun ending.

Circle work needs to be regular to be effective, the more frequently it takes place the more the children will speak out and air their views. Circle-Time is about giving responsibility to children and will take place at least once a week, but ideally every day.

Ideas for Circle-Time Activities

1. Simon says.

2. Number game. Each person has a number. Call your own number and one other:

10-3, 3-14, 14-20, etc

3. Game to change seats.

Move chairs – anyone who likes chips etc.

Discuss need for control/care – no bumping etc.

Discuss need for honesty.

4. Tell a good tale – use the round: "I would like to say well done to .... because you..."

Children may not nominate their best friend.

5. Children nominate others for improvement in work or behaviour.

6. Children nominate themselves for improvements in work or behaviour.

7. In pairs – say what you like about the person.

8. Wink murder.

9. Pass round rainstorm – finger wriggling, thigh slapping, (thunder), smile, (sunshine).

10. Looking skills. Children paired. They look carefully at each other. One changes his/her appearance slightly while the other looks away. The change (ie sleeves pushed up) to be noticed by the other child.

Ideas for discussion, etc during Circle-Time Work

Circle work should begin positively, eg congratulating children on ability to organise circle.

How do you feel if you make a mistake?

Why do you need to make mistakes?

What do others do to make you feel worse?

What do others do to make you feel better?

Congratulations for: the way you are listening, sitting straight in your chairs, still and calm, looking at the talker.

What makes you feel fed up?

How do you feel when called a name?

Saying sorry to people?

Children bring their work and post-its.

GOLDEN RULES

Each teacher will formulate with the children Golden Rules (practical and behavioural) for their classroom e.g.

What do we need in this class in order for us to learn well and get on well together?

These to be regularly referred to and reviewed/assessed.

These should be displayed.

Golden Rules drawn up with children

We decided together:

Do understand it is alright to make mistakes. Do not tease anyone who does.

Be kind, be honest and truthful. Do not lie or cheat.

Do be gentle. Do not push and shove.

Do be polite. Do not all talk at once.

Do be a friend. Do not call a person names, unless they like the name.

Do share with everybody you can – do not leave anyone out, be a friend.

Do listen to each other. Do not interrupt.

Do follow instructions. Do not disobey.

Do concentrate on work. Do not give up

INCENTIVES

All adults will:

Trust, listen, give a chance, encourage, praise, like, every child.

If a child does something wrong the child will know that it is the behaviour that is disliked and not him/her.

Treat with courtesy, e.g. not raise voice.

Be consistent.

Recognise children's fears.

Be positive.

Show we care.

Not jump to conclusions, but deal with each incident afresh.

Help children understand that their fears, difficulties, etc are not unique.

Appreciate how well children cope with their personal problems.

Make early use of the hairy eyeball (a stern warning look.)

Parents will hear regular "good news" about their child via our incentive systems:

    Responsibilities with badges, eg chief gardener
    Swimming ribbons
    Sharing work with another audience
    Displaying work
    Physical contact
    Comments on Post its
    Comments on Reading Diaries
    Verbal comments to parents
    Inviting parents in to see work
    Stickers awarded by adults or other children for behaviour and work
    Praise awarded by adults or other children for behaviour and work
    Working alongside children and recognising mutual differences
    Sharing outside interests
    Children helping each other
    Self-esteem certificates
    Recognising the value of mistakes
    "Tell a nice tale"
    Ladder sheets as individuals behaviour or work targets.

Possible Strategies

'Do not disturb' notices – teachers could use these to ensure they have uninterrupted talking time with individual children.

Every child should have a turn at responsibility, eg taking the register, helping younger children.

Creating privileges. Creating Privilege-Time.

All children will receive each term at least one certificate and three stickers. All class teachers will keep a check list.

Target Ladders or Pictures

These are a means by which the children can self-improve. Each child has a chart and identifies their own target (something attainable.) Children are responsible for their own charts. They colour in a space for each successful attempt at target. At the end of each week they have their ladder/picture signed by a teacher or assistant. When it is completed the child may choose whether to take it home or to the headteacher.

SANCTIONS

Teachers will have clear privileges which are offered to children, but can be withdrawn if any of the Golden Rules are broken, eg sitting next to friends.

If a child misbehaves with a supply teacher one written warning is to be given on an individual piece of paper. On second misbehaviour the child is requested to take the piece of paper to the head. If the child refuses, send piece of paper via messenger.

DINNER TIME POLICY

Dinner time affects children. Their self-esteem can be radically lowered. It can also create problems which interrupt the children's learning.

The Supervisors are in two teams, each with a team leader.

Lisa Mollart	Team Leader	**Cath Smedley**
Angela Downard		Joan Whale
Pam Butcher		Louise Morgan

Each team will supervise either the playground or hall and change venues at 12.30.

Each team will alternate weekly their original starting point.

First Sitting Jobs

Put out sandwich boxes

Water

Put away comics, carpets and playground box.

Second Sitting Jobs

Take out comics and carpets

Playground box

Put away tables and chairs

At 12.59 the team leader will blow the whistle and the children will line up in classes

Children in the playground use Upper School toilets. Children may not re-enter school without permission.

Wet Dinner Time

Children must be sitting down in their classrooms.

Children may use only what the teacher has provided, report if more is needed.

MDSA's will supervise throughout the whole of dinner time in the following areas:

Lower School	Hall	Upper school
Louise Morgan	Angie Downard	Pam Butcher
Cath Smedley	Joan Whale	Lisa Mollart

Fire Alarm

In case of fire alarm, all children should exit from the nearest door and assemble in the playground.

Injuries

If a child has a minor injury attend to it. If you need expert advise ask Mrs Owen. If there is a possible major injury, send for Mary Smith.

General Safety Rules

Children are expected to walk when inside the building. Running, jostling and overtaking are not acceptable.

Queuing Policy

A few children are let in at a time. One MDSA supervises by the courtyard door and one at hall door.

Policy regarding children who may not have enough food:

1. Quietly whisper "I happen to have some spare sandwiches, do you want one?"

2. Tell Class Teacher.

Sanctions

Initial Offence	1 verbal warning

For Misbehaviour in Line

Initial Offence	Standing against wall and write their name in the book, sent in when MDSA chooses.
Repeat Offence	Child sent to team leader, name written down in book.
Third Offence	Child sent to Headteacher

This would be by-passed in extreme behaviour and child sent straight to headteacher.

Incentives

Praise

Praising child to that child's teacher

Stickers

Lunchtime helper badges – for reward. Helpers will do jobs and play with lonely children, patrol toilets and quiet area.

Table of the week

Dinner Time Certificates - once a half term to everybody whose name has not been written in a book.

MDSA's are allocated to particular classes so they can build a two way relationship with class teachers. Teachers will inform them of children who need particular care and MDSA's will inform class teachers of concerns and children's behaviour good and bad.

Headteacher will

Invite all staff including MDSA's, kitchen staff, caretaker to a once termly assembly near the beginning of term.

Have regular half termly meetings to review the policy and assess children on behaviour flow charts.

Call regular meetings for footballers and take minutes.

Provide each class with a box of equipment for use only at dinner time.

Will remind children of dinner time policy particularly:

> playing nicely
>
> good table manners
>
> walking in corridor
>
> hands-up system
>
> sanctions and incentives

See kitchen staff regularly to enquire on good/bad behaviour.

Help to raise the status of MDSA's.

Teachers will

Teach playground games during P.E. once a term.

Regularly discuss dinnertime during Circle-Time work, which may take the following structure:-

1. Tell a good tale about someone else (not a best friend)

2. Someone I need to say sorry to.

3. Something I am pleased with about myself - concerning dinner time.

Write a list for wet dinner time showing what can and cannot be used.

Check wet dinner time box once a half term.

Talk to their MDSA at least once a week.

Help to raise the status of MDSA's.

MDSA's will

Have lunchtime helper badges.

Have a quiet area (indoor if cold).

Have a quiet area box containing comics and drawing equipment.

Have carpet squares.

Use "hands-up" – for praise as well as criticism.

Look for the positive behaviours and give stickers.

Have a collection of cardboard boxes.

Where appropriate, play games or organise a lunchtime helper to do so, eg. treasure hunt game.

Help to raise the self-esteem of the children.

Give out dinner time certificates to their class each term.

Behaviour we wish to discourage

Bad language.

Ruining of other children's games.

Hurting each other's feelings, e.g. name calling.

Hurting each other physically.

Bad table manners.

Behaviour we wish to encourage through incentive system

Politeness, good table manners.

A gentle, caring attitude.

Helpfulness.

Following instructions.

Children beyond normal incentives and sanctions

Need to have specific contract drawn up with MDSA and teacher.

Strategies for MDSA's

Importance of giving a warning look.

Importance of keeping voice low and not shouting.

Take time to talk:

i) to individual children you are worried about

ii) to teachers and headteacher about individual children.

Football Policy

Upper School children and Lower School children will choose two Captains each, every half term.

Before the choice of Captain imade, children will be reminded of the qualities which make a good School Captain, e.g.:-

People who choose equal girls and boys.

People who chose people with good skills.

People who need to improve their skills.

Fairness.

People who feel they can make mistakes.

Captains will then select teams. The team lists will then be typed and displayed in each classroom with a copy given to each MDSA.

CONTRACTING

This procedure is for children who have not responded to the usual sanctions and incentives. It is important that the rest of the class should be a part of the contract – they could give a sticker, clap or help with the time watching.

The class also has to have re-enforcements or treats when supporting a child on contract. This raises the child's popularity as s/he is seen as the instigator of the "treat". This changes the child's self-image so that eventually s/he perceives themselves as worthwhile.

Skills of effective contracting

Identify with the child, actual behaviour(s) that need to be discouraged and behaviour that needs to be encouraged (target).

Discuss with child what the positive pay off will be – is this better than the previous negative one? What would be, for the child, a very good immediate re-enforcement? Working with the other children towards agreed re-enforcement.

Points to remember:

1. Target, to begin with, must be small and attainable.

2. Re-enforcement must be daily.

3. The aim of target is to widen it to share with all.

4. Contract needs constant assessment – contract changing needs to have all members of staff notified.

An example of a contract is shown below

Contract

We agree that if G can do what he is asked to do by his teacher when the clock is on for half an hour twice a day, he will get a special time with Bob from 2.30 - 3.00pm each day.

Signed   Pupil   ....

         Teacher   ....

The Contract was drawn up after considering the following:

When did G look vaguely happy? When in a one to one situation.

What is the home situation like?

What the world looks like from the child's point of view.

Why should he trust adults – none had been trustworthy?

The perceived pay off for negative behaviour – funny noises, challenging adult's authority, getting power back and self-esteem.

G seems to need calm concentration to find his interests

As G gets more confident another child needs to join him so it does not become a dependent relationship. Bring more children, eventually Bob goes into class.

The Contract was drawn up with the child, caretaker and class teacher. It is crucial that contracts are typed and signed and the teacher keeps strictly to the agreement.

Development

In this case the child's targets could be increased and eventually the stage could be reached of daily good behaviour assessed by the child.

STAFF SUPPORT

At least one staff meeting a term will be held to firstly share strategies that have created success, and secondly, to discuss anxieties. Staff need to look at children's inner worlds with the help of the Maslow model.

- Remember – The Golden Purse, every child needs:

  Praise

  Recognition

  Affection

  Success

- Bragging masks low self-esteem

- Those with good self-esteem can cope with a bad day because they have a full purse to draw on.

- Children with low self-esteem are generally disruptive or withdrawn.

- Staff must share the load and get a break.

- When things start going wrong staff need to look into the world of a child. We all need to keep morale high by continuing to share bad days in a culture of honesty. Appreciate we are a good team and recognise strengths in each other.

- There are three booklets for Circle-Time ideas available in the staff room.

- The quality of behaviour and learning in the school is continually improving. It is very important that all staff appreciate their successes and look after their own self-esteem. They must say to themselves:

"I have done this –
I have survived well!!"

Appendix 2

Initial Circle-Time Sessions in progress

INITIAL CIRCLE-TIME IN PROGRESS

The formulation of a class's Golden Rules is fundamental to the successful development of a whole school policy. This section begins with quite detailed notes on sessions to help children consider Golden Rules. The notes were made by teachers observing the author as she lead some initial Circle-Time Sessions.

THE SCHOOL OF KIND MAGIC – FOR YEAR 4 CHILDREN

In the circle Jenny explained that when she put on a piece of costume it was a signal that she was going to act. Then Jenny put on a cloak and pretended to be a kind magician reading out a mimed letter written to her. "Dear Miss Magic Kindness, please will you make a spell so that my mummy does not have to wash up again". She pretended to pin up the letter then told the children that she was welcoming new children to her school of kind magic. Jenny told the children they had been chosen to attend because they had all written her the wonderful letters she was holding in her hand. "Now who wrote this letter to me about her mummy wanting help with the washing up?"

Child puts up hand. "That was so kind" said Jenny. She then asked children what kind of spells they would like to send to Miss Magic Kindness. Quickly the children volunteered such things as:–

"help my young sister to learn the ABC"
"help my brother be kinder to me"
"make the car better for mummy"

An imaginary cauldron was placed in the centre of the circle. Jenny asked what did they think the cauldron looked like. Suggestions offered included:–

"silver"
"a boat"
"like a magic box"

Jenny told the children she needed to put beautiful things in the cauldron to make kind magic "I've just put in a golden butterfly. What else can I use?"

"silver bird"
"stripey rose"
"fluffy teddy"
"rainbow leaf"

Jenny took up a silver wand and dipped it into the imaginary cauldron. She asked for magic words which they all said together.

"abra cadabra"
"hocus pocus"

She then waved the wand over the children, sprinkling magic dust over them "Now you are spacemen on the moon."

All mimed being spacemen within the circle. The children were then given a turn with the cloak and wand making spells on their own and changing the whole class and Jenny into...

"jumping rabbits"
"fairies"

After each spell Jenny congratulated each magician saying "you must be very kind, because spells only work for kind people." So everyone clapped the child.

Then Jenny asked children what the most important 'magic' ingredient in friendship is:

"kindness"

"Why is kindness important?"

"because it makes you feel good"
"because it helps people"
"it's nice to be kind"

"Do we want any Golden Rules in this class to help people be nice to each other?" Jenny and children decide on a Golden Rule.

Do Be Kind to People

The session ended with a hand squeeze of kindness around the circle.

THE SHY RABBIT – FOR RECEPTION CHILDREN

Jenny produced a rabbit puppet that 'talked' to children.

"I am very shy but I heard that children are very clever and I needed some help so I've been very brave and come up here to talk to you. First of all I need to know how clever you are so I've brought my friend little talking Ted. (Rabbit bring out small teddy). When I give him to someone it's their time to guess the name of an animal in my school and no one can interrupt. If you don't want to guess you can just say 'pass'".

'Ted' was given to a child and as it went round each one said the name of an animal – Rabbit nods vigorously and a few said 'pass' or repeated a name of an animal (still Rabbit nods vigorously).

When it came back around, Rabbit took Ted back and jumped up and down delightedly – "Oooh now I know you are very clever I know you can help me with my problem, the thing is..." (Rabbit pulls her ears down and looks very uncomfortable) "er... I love my new school and my teacher... and all the dinner ladies... but when I go out at lunchtime I get really sad... can you guess why?"

Children said

> "You get pushed over"
> "People won't play with you"
> "Nobody will be your friend"
> "You get called horrible names"
> "You get called spotty
>> stupid
>> big ears
>> idiot
>> "a horrible "f" word"

"Oh" says Rabbit "you guessed exactly what happened to me, but also there's another little animal out there who's especially horrible to me... he's called Hedgehog. He gets people to call me names, tells friends not to let me in, he frightens me, would you be very brave and talk to him for me?"

All children shot their hands up and shouted yes (you could almost hear "lynch him"!!)

"Ah" says, Rabbit "but what will you do?"

"Hit him back"
"Call him names"

"Oh dear, I don't think that'll work because I know he's got a big brother at home that does that and it makes him worse... What else could you do?"

"Tell him"
"Talk to him"

"Oh that sounds great. I'll go and hide." Out comes hedgehog.

"Well, what do you want?" says hedgehog.

"You have been horrible" say the children.

Hedgehog answers: "No, I haven't. I haven't pushed him over or hurt him"

"No, but you called him names"
"You left him out of games"

"Oh dear! so did I hurt him?"

"Yes – his feelings"

"Oh is there anything I can do to make it better?"

"Be his friend"
"Play games with him"
"Be nice to him"

"I'm just an animal – I don't know about these things – Is there a Golden Rule that I can take back to my school to help the animals be nice to each other?"

After some discussion the children decided on two Golden Rules

Do ask people to join in — don't leave anyone out
Do say nice things to people – don't say nasty things

Jenny then brought back Rabbit and Hedgehog tapped him on the shoulder and said "Sorry... please will you be my friend" Rabbit was delighted... and then the children taught the two of them some playground games they can play together.

THINKING TOGETHER ABOUT LUNCHTIME
– FOR YEAR 5 CHILDREN

Jenny started by playing a game called 'Mix'em up' (see p.122) – not only did this mix up the children – but in the excitement to gain a chair they were pushing and shoving each other.

Once they had a chair Jenny then asked the children "When do you feel pushed around or hurt in school?" Children's answers included:

"In the playground"

"Coming into school after playtime"

"Standing in the line"

Carrying on with the 'talking object' a brass egg, was passed around the circle and each child was given the opportunity to volunteer information of what hurts their feelings during playtime. They were told not to mention anyone's name, but could say 'somebody.'

Children suggested:

"Being kicked"

"Being punched"

"Name calling"

"Being horrid to someone"

"People not letting you join in their games"

Jenny then asked the children to be honest and put their hands up if they hurt other people's feelings. Many put their hands up and they were praised for their honesty.

Jenny asked if the children wanted any Golden Rules to encourage positive behaviour. Children volunteered several suggestions, discussed these and put forward two Golden Rules.

Say kind things to one another.

Ask people to join in.

The Circle-Time Session ended with a game of "Follow the Leader" where everyone could join in and have fun together.

KEEPER OF THE KEYS – FOR YEAR 3 CHILDREN

Using a game, Jenny and the children made up a story. A chair was placed in the centre, with a bunch of keys to represent treasure. The children decided that the treasure was a gold basket of golden bananas, rubies and diamonds. The treasure belonged to the Golden Banana King who was kind and gave everyone a piece of his treasure. One night a tame lion with a collar of golden bananas came and took the treasure. They decided the lion had been hypnotised by a wicked man and made it steal the treasure to give it to him. What sort of person would this be? –"greedy", "selfish", "mean", "uncaring."

The wicked man hides in a cave and makes a trap to prevent people finding him. He makes "a high rock outside the cave", "an icy step" and "a wall of fire". What shall we call this man? "Orange Warrior". He wants to set up another tribe of greedy, nasty people, so what sort of rules would they have on Orange Island and Banana Island? The children suggested a lot of anti-social rules.

What things do we like most in people? "kindness" "caring" "being helpful" "sharing". Children passed round the keys – i.e.. the "banana crown" and when a child had this s/he said a kind thing they had done that week. These things become objects placed around the circle.

Jenny asked "what sort of person would they choose to recapture the Banana King's treasure, children volunteered, "brave", "good", "kind".

Then Jenny explained how the story could be made into a game. A child played the Orange Warrior and sat on a chair in the centre, blindfolded. A chair is placed in the circle to represent the high rock, a tray was put down for the 'icy step' and an upturned chair represented the wall of fire. The chosen child attempted to negotiate the obstacles and creep up to the chair and 'capture' the keys (placed beside it). If the Orange Warrior thinks s/he hears the intruder he is allowed to say 'stop' and point in the direction of the noise. If correct another child is chosen to recapture the treasure.

Jenny asked "How did you help someone capture the treasure?"

"I stayed quiet."

Jenny asked, "If the treasure was a target, what would you like to achieve at school?"

"maths and writing"
"reading"
"swimming"
"working and writing"

"What can stop you from concentrating?" asked Jenny.

"people talking"
"noise"
"being interrupted"

Jenny asked "who can be honest and say if they do any of these things?" Many children put up their hands to talk about the things they do to annoy other people.

"Shall we make some Golden Rules to help us concentrate?" asked Jenny.

Children suggested:

Do work quietly and do concentrate and work calmly

The children decided they'd like to make 'Do Not Disturb' signs to put on their desks when they want to concentrate on their work.